BODY LANGUAGE

How to Detect High-Stakes Liars Through Body Language Analysis and Everything You Need to Influence People with Emotional Intelligence, Powerful Communication and Persuasion

By

Blake Reyes

is the solitary and utter responsibility of the recipient reader. Under no circumstances will any legal responsibility or blame be held against the publisher for any reparation, damages, or monetary loss due to the information herein, either directly or indirectly.

Respective authors own all copyrights not held by the publisher.

The information herein is offered for informational purposes solely, and is universal as so. The presentation of the information is without contract or any type of guarantee assurance.

The trademarks that are used are without any consent, and the publication of the trademark is without permission or backing by the trademark owner. All trademarks and brands within this book are for clarifying purposes only and are the owned by the owners themselves, not affiliated with this document.

TABLE OF CONTENTS

INTRODUCTION 9

CHAPTER 1 - BEING A LIE DETECTOR 11

CHAPTER 2 - FOOLPROOF STEPS TO DISCOVER
LIARS 17

CHAPTER 3 - SENSING LIES, AND MOST
COMMON SIGNS SOMEONE IS LYING TO YOU....... 22

CHAPTER 4 - CLUES TO REVEAL TRUE
INTENTIONS 28

CHAPTER 5 - HOW TO DISCOVER DARK
PEOPLE'S MASKS... 37

CHAPTER 6 - THE POKER FACE MYTHS 42

CHAPTER 7 - HOW TO UNDERSTAND AN
HONEST EMOTION VS. FAKE AND
MANIPULATED EMOTIONS...................................... 45

CHAPTER 8 - WHEN THE LIE HITS HOME 49

CHAPTER 9 - THE POWER OF EMOTIONAL
INTELLIGENCE 56

What is Emotional Intelligence? 57

Hallmarks of the Emotional Mind 61

Busting The Myths About Emotional
Intelligence.. 72

CHAPTER 10 - SCHOOLING THE EMOTIONS 76

What Is Emotion?.. 78

Why Do We Need Emotions? 79

Why Are Some People More Emotional Than
Others?... 83

The Roots of Empathy 86

Managing with Heart..88

How to Get the Best out of People 94

CHAPTER 11 - THE ART OF PERSUASION.................98

Psychological Trick to Get People to Say Yes 104

How to build lasting Relationships 107

CHAPTER 12 - SOCIAL INFLUENCE 113

CHAPTER 13 - THE ART OF BODY LANGUAGE 124

The Five C's of Body Language 128

Mastering the Secrets of Non-Verbal

Communication 129

How to Interpret Verbal Communication 132

CHAPTER 14 - THE SUBCONSCIOUS MIND AND

THE LIMBIC BRAIN SYSTEM 138

How to Speed-Read People...............................142

The most powerful techniques you can use

to fake your body language and manipulate

Anyone's 150

How to Influence and Subdue the Mind 153

CHAPTER 15 - HOW TO USE SUBLIMINAL

MESSAGES AND HOW TO USE THEM TO

MANIPULATE PEOPLE..162

How to Decode Micro Expressions....................165

Body Language Mistakes to Avoid.....................178

CONCLUSION 184

INTRODUCTION

A lot of research has shown that as much as 80% of our communication is through body language and facial expressions. By understanding our body language, we will understand what signals we send to the environment. Through the body, we give people what we think and feel without even being aware of it. By becoming aware of other people's body language, we can understand when someone is lying to us or giving us signals that they are attracted to us. Even with people who are in a relationship, the success of the relationship may depend on the ability to send and receive signals.

This is because it is sometimes much easier for partners to point out some problems or wishes in a non-verbal way than by speaking. When they see the person who is attracted to them, people automatically start to raise or lower their eyebrows slightly. Such a reaction takes only a fraction of a second, but if we pay attention to our own or others' behavior, we will see that it is easily noticeable and true. A raised eyebrow 100% proves that we are sexually attracted to someone.

By adjusting their clothes, men want to draw attention to themselves, while playing with buttons shows nervousness. Psychologists say it can also be a subconscious sign that a man wants to undress in front of a woman. The attitude in which a man takes off his jacket and places his hands on his hips is a clear sign that he already has concrete plans with the woman who is attracted to him. Playing with hair is a technique used by women.

By removing the hair from her face, she subconsciously lets the man know that she wants to get closer and get to know him more closely, and conveys the same message with a slight lick of her lips. In this document, you will learn a lot about body language, some tricks, and tips to get started.

CHAPTER 1

BEING A LIE DETECTOR

Tim Roth, who we know from Quentin Tarantino's 1995 movie The Four Rooms, starring in a jog, also starred in the Lie to Me series of Human Lie Detector, which encouraged me to explore human body language. So-called non-verbal communication. It has been communicated in this way since the beginning of time. It is a very important form of communication, and today many are not aware of it.

Ignorance is sometimes bliss. After acquiring this knowledge, you may be hurt when it is obvious that someone is lying to you. Various deception techniques are used by police, forensics, psychologists, security experts, and other investigators. This information is also useful for administrators, employers, as well as everyone for use in daily circumstances where separating truth from lies will prevent anyone from falling victim to fraud and other deception.

Signs of deception can be seen if one's behavior is limited and rigid, with very little movement. The liar holds his hands to his body, trying to take up as little space as possible. He avoids eye contact with the

11

person he is lying to or stares at him without blinking. His hands touch his face, throat, and mouth. Also, he touches or rubs his nose, ear...

A contradiction in the expression of emotional gestures can be observed like a forced fake smile. The display of emotions is delayed, the reaction stays longer, then stops at once. Time is excluded between emotions and gestures, expressions, and words. For example, someone says, "I like it!" when receiving a gift, and then he smiles after that statement. Gestures or expressions do not respond to verbal statements, such as when someone says, "I love you" while frowning. Expressions are limited to mouth gestures if anyone fakes emotions (happiness, surprise, sadness, awe) instead of the whole face. Let's say when someone smiles, of course, the whole face is on—the jaw expands into a smile, the cheek is raised, the eyes and forehead are wrinkled down, etc.

Interaction and reaction - The culprit defends himself, while the innocent person responds more often with the attack. A liar is uncomfortable when confronted and often turns his head or body away from an interviewer. He unwittingly places objects (a book, a coffee cup) between himself and you, as a symbolic obstacle.

Other Signs of Lying - If you think someone is lying, then quickly change the topic of conversation, the liar will accompany you voluntarily and become more relaxed. The culprit wants the subject of the conversation to be something else, while the innocent person may be confused by the sudden change of topic and will probably want you to go back to the previous one. The use of humor or sarcasm is often used by liars to avoid talking about a particular topic.

Micro-expressions - are instant involuntary facial expressions that are drawn on people's faces when they hide emotions without even being aware of it. They are characterized by speed and tension. They occur in a split second and disappear just as quickly. They are reluctant to move facial muscles because we cannot influence them by our will.

They are usually grouped into seven universal emotions: anger, disgust, fear, sadness, happiness, surprise, and contempt.

Micro-expressions give us away when we lie. If we try to hide emotions with a fake smile, we give off hidden emotions to the involuntary movements of the facial muscles. They only show how one feels, which does not lead to the conclusion that one is a liar; they only show one's current emotional state.

13

(If someone saw a picture of a dog and commented that it was great and that the dog was beautiful, and the expression on the face at the time depicted disgust, it might not be a lie. Maybe that person was bitten by the dog, so the picture reminded him of that situation.)

Eyes - Eyes are a mirror of the soul, more accurately reflecting our current emotional state, the state of mind. Some scientific studies say that people unconsciously look in certain directions during the conversation and that it has to do with lying, remembering, imagining, because certain centers in the brain respond differently to certain stimuli, and this is reflected in the eye muscle. The analysis of one's diversion is not reliable to conclude as to whether one is lying or not, but it is certainly interesting. Try it.

Visually Constructed Images - If someone told you to imagine a purple boar with green tufts, as you visually construct that image, your eyes would look upwards to the right.

Visually Memorized Pictures - If someone asked you what color the house you once lived in as you try to remember, your eyes would look up to the left.

Sound Construction - When you try to imagine a sound you haven't heard before, your eyes will be pointing to the right.

Sound Recall - Remember the voice of your acquaintance, eyes will look to the left.

Feeling - Remembering the smell of a campfire will direct your gaze down to the right, as well as thinking about taste, emotion, or smell.

Inner conversation - When a person is thinking, thinking, talking to himself in his head, his eyes are directed down to the left.

Of course, when looking at the interviewee, the left is right, right is left, as in a mirror. This is true for right-handed people, and the situation is the opposite for left-handed people. If someone is staring at you in a non-moving eye, this can also be a sign of lying. All this through analysis and examples has proven more accurate than incorrect.

It is very important that body language can also be misinterpreted. Therefore, some of the ways we can apply in most cases are listed. Body language is viewed comprehensively, and we need to know one's normal behavior to notice deviations. It is not enough for someone to blink repeatedly and to think that he

15

is impatient, insecure, or lying. Verbal speech, tone, and other things should also be included so that we can more easily assess a particular situation. Sometimes people are uncomfortable with their skin, they are unsure of themselves, some inconvenience has happened, something bothers them, and maybe they care about you, their job, etc. We cannot judge others just like that unless we know the whole story, but these gestures can also help us understand the other side.

CHAPTER 2

FOOLPROOF STEPS TO DISCOVER LIARS

Some signs can help to identify when a person is lying because when a lie is told, the body shows small signs that are difficult to avoid, even in the case of experienced liars.

So, to know if someone is lying, it is important to pay attention to various details in the eyes, face, breath, and even in the hands or arms. The following are some techniques to find out if one is telling you a lie:

1. Look closely at the face

While a smile can easily help hide a lie, there are small facial expressions that can indicate that the person is lying. For example, when the cheeks become redder during the conversation, it is a sign that the person is anxious and this can be a sign that he is telling something that is not true or that it makes him uncomfortable to talk about it. Also, other signs such as dilating your nostrils while breathing, breathing deeply, biting your lips, or blinking your eyes too quickly may indicate that your brain is working too hard to build a false story.

2. Observe all body movements

This is one of the most critical steps in figuring out whether somebody's lying and is being used by specialists in lie detection. Normally, when we're honest, the whole body works in a coordinated fashion, but when we want to trick others, it's normal not to synchronize it. The person can speak very confidently, for example, but his body is withdrawn, contradicting the feeling the voice gives. The most popular body language changes that suggest a lie is being told include being very quiet throughout the conversation, crossing your arms, and holding your hands behind your back.

3. Watch your hands

One may most likely observe the whole body to know when someone is lying, but the movement of the hands can be enough to discover a liar. This is because while trying to tell a lie, the mind is concerned with keeping the body's movement closer to the natural, but the movement of the hands is very difficult to copy.

Thus, hand movement can indicate:

Hands closed: it can be a sign of a lack of honesty or excessive stress;

Hands touching clothes: shows that the person is uncomfortable and anxious;

Moving your hands, a lot without need: it is a movement often done by someone who is used to lying.

Put your hands on the back of your neck or neck: shows anxiety and discomfort with what you are talking about. Also, placing objects in front of the person you are talking to can be a sign that you are lying, as it shows a desire to create distance, which usually happens when we tell something that makes us nervous and uncomfortable.

4. Listen to everything very carefully

Changes in voice can quickly identify a liar, especially when sudden changes in tone of voice occur, such as speaking in a thick voice and then starting to speak in a thinner voice. But in some situations, it may be more difficult to detect these changes, and thus it is, therefore, important to be aware of any changes in pace that occur while speaking.

5. Pay attention to your eyes

It is possible to learn a great deal about the feelings of a person only through their eyes. This is likely because the majority of people are conditioned unconsciously to look in those directions contrary to what they think or feel.

The types of looks generally related to a lie include:

Look up and left: it happens when you realize you're talking about a lie;

Look left: it's more normal when you're trying to create a lie when you're talking;

Look down and left: it indicates you're worried about something that's been accomplished. Other signals that can be transmitted by the eyes, and that can indicate a lie, include looking directly into the eyes for most of the conversation and blinking more often than normal.

That's right, whoever is telling you a lie, uses as much detail as he can, in the mistaken belief of being more credible. The liar fills his story with many (unnecessary) details. What we have to do then is to be continuous with questions that lead you to contradict yourself to lose the line of speech.

So how should you act if you have a liar in front of you? Well, that depends on the case. In fights between coworkers or in fights between couples, what you could do is perhaps ask some general questions that cannot be answered with a resounding "yes" or "no" and then ask more specific questions. But it takes a lot of work. Perhaps it is better to trust the sixth sense itself, which rarely fails, in addition to asking yourself if you would be ready for the truth and, if you would not be being deceived in the face of evident lies. Also, some believe in their lies. And what would be the truth? Follow your heart.

CHAPTER 3

SENSING LIES, AND MOST COMMON SIGNS SOMEONE IS LYING TO YOU

1. Pinocchio poses

You can be a very attentive and insightful person, but your chances of catching a liar in the act are relatively low. This has to do with the psychology of lying and body language. A layman in body language usually hits only 50% of the time when he tries to identify a liar by his posture. But not even the greatest experts are always right: your chances of success are usually around 65% or a little more. The main difficulty lies in the fact that the signs of lying are often confused with traces of shyness, anxiety, and nervousness. It is what Camargo calls "Othello's mistake," about the classic Shakespeare character. Instead of fear, the protagonist of the tragedy sees betrayal in the eyes of his wife, Desdemona, and commits a terrible injustice. In real life, miscalculations are also often frequent—especially if you are emotionally involved in the situation. The advantage of the expert who analyzes videos or interviews defendants, for example, is that he does not have a direct relationship with the liar.

In everyday work, however, the feelings and expectations you have about your interlocutor can "cloud" your judgment about his honesty—for better or worse. Still, certain classic signs often betray liars.

2. Cover your mouth

A typical gesture of someone who is not telling the truth is to touch their mouth. Stroking your chin, wiping your lips with your fingers, placing a pencil or other object in front of your mouth are very common signs. The concern with the mouth reflects the desire to prevent others from hearing the lie that will be uttered, or even the unconscious desire to suppress their own words, because they are false.

3. Avoid eye contact

Not looking directly into the other's eyes does not necessarily mean lack of sincerity: it may simply be insecurity or shyness. Still, it is common for the liar to lower his eyes to prevent the falsity of his statements from being perceived. However, this detail can be tricky. Many liars, knowing this, do exactly the opposite when they lie: they look directly into the victim's eyes in an attempt to make their statements more credible.

4. Compress the lips

A liar in action usually closes in on himself, preventing words from coming out of his mouth. A very clear sign of this resistance to communication is to fold your lips inward, squeezing them tightly. This is a common reaction to questions with the potential to expose the truth. The "disappearance" of the lips can indicate that the person was affected by the question and does not want to answer it.

5. Look up and to the right

When looking at the upper right corner, the individual usually wants to create an image. This is one of the most consistent signs of lying—the person makes a creative effort, that is, prepares something fictitious to say. Many individuals turn their heads in the same direction. In many cases, looking away also serves not to face the interlocutor directly.

6. Show micro-wrinkles on the forehead

The nervousness caused by the situation can also cause the appearance of small horizontal wrinkles on the liar's forehead. The problem is that they disappear very quickly and are not always easy to observe. But be careful: the lines on the forehead often reflect a kind of tension that has nothing to do with lies. In general, wrinkles that denote mere nervousness are well pronounced and remain on the other person's face for longer.

7. Restrict hand and arm movements

It is common for people who lack the truth to decrease their gesticulation greatly. "The hands are stuck to the legs, in the pockets, placed behind," writes an expert. "The movements are scarce and controlled." The reason for this paralysis is unconscious: without knowing it, the person believes that the more immobile he is, the more easily he will go unnoticed by the attentive gaze of his interlocutor. He also tries to reduce his body language so as not to let his gestures end up contradicting his speech.

8. Rigid and repetitive movements

In an attempt to close in on his own body, the insincere individual will tend to move in a hard, repetitive, and mechanical way. The more intense these gestures, the more it becomes clear that the liar is uncomfortable and wages an internal struggle to keep control of the situation.

9. Shrink your head

The liar tends to retract his own body: shrunken neck, low chin, legs together, and crossed arms indicate an unconscious attempt to control his own emotions. The behavior goes back to cave times. In the face of a predator, prehistoric man had three options: flee, fight, or be paralyzed. The third option is the one that draws the least attention. Not for nothing, the liar who wants to "survive" his interlocutor tries to shrink himself in all possible ways.

10. Often touching one's own body

Self-hugging and caressing your arms can denote insecurity, anxiety, the need for protection, and unconscious return to a childlike posture. There are several touches to the body itself that betray liars. Running your hands over your legs to get rid of imaginary dirt, for example, can denote worry and anxiety. Scratching the nose is another characteristic gesture, says an expert: During his testimony in the Monica Lewinsky case, former US President Bill Clinton touched his nose more than 25 times.

11. Shrug only one shoulder

This is one of the most classic signs of lying, according to the American psychologist Paul Ekman, considered one of the world's greatest specialists in facial and body expressions. The posture of the individual who lacks the truth is asymmetrical: one of his shoulders stands up or protrudes slightly forward. With the gesture, he tries to convey disregard and little concern for what he is saying. Often, this disguised tone of disdain also appears in the liar's voice.

12. Trying to get away from the caller

One of the techniques most used by experts to unmask a liar is to get as close as possible to him during a delicate question. This tactic can make him more anxious and prone to surrender. This is because the more removed he can be from the other, the more secure he will feel. The attempt to maintain a comfortable distance appears both physically and verbally: he will also try to stay away from the thorniest details in his story. Still, you need to be careful with that sign. Certain liars get very close to their victims.

CHAPTER 4

CLUES TO REVEAL TRUE INTENTIONS

It is not always in the process of conversation that you can learn about the true intentions of a person. What words are silent about can be told by the eyes, facial expressions, behavior, and gestures of the interlocutor.

How to know a person's intentions?

The first way: ask him about it. A person can tell the truth or can be a deceiver. So, there is no guarantee to hear the truth on the question asked.

The second way: to catch and remember the first opinion of a person when meeting. Intuition will not deceive us. If there is a negative impression—wait for the trick. People at a subconscious level recognize signals using gestures, postures, facial expressions.

The third way. Observe the look of the interlocutor. Running eyes betray shame, fear, or deceit. The excessive shine of the eyes will warn about the excitement of a person; perhaps he is in a state of alcoholic or drug intoxication. Dilated pupils are a sign of pleasure or intense experience. The random movement of the pupils occurs when intoxicated. The faster they move, the stronger the interlocutor is drunk. Frequent blinking can be observed to deceive you.

The interlocutor, who prefers to look you in the eye, intends to lie or not to say anything. If he has something to hide, then he will not be completely frank with you. A "drilling" gaze can give out an intention to surpass you and dominate you not only in conversation.

A direct look into the interlocutor's eyes is not always a guarantee of honest intentions. It often happens that professional cheaters spend hours honing their skills in front of a mirror. They easily control their eyes, facial expressions, and make sure that their hands do not touch their faces.

If a person is inherently shy, he will not look into the eyes when communicating. His speech may be confused, and his eyes involuntarily "run" around. The modest man has no bad intentions, and his behavior is due to a special mental organization. True, to recognize this feature, you need to be familiar with it for more than a single day.

The fourth way, the last. Closed poses (crossing arms or legs), touching during a conversation to a person, confused and incoherent speech will give the indication that he intends to lie or not to say something. Transferring from a topic you are interested in another is a signal; the interlocutor wants to escape from the discussion of an unpleasant topic for him.

Be observant with new people, but do not lose your vigilance with old friends. Perhaps you continue to communicate with them only through ignorance of their intentions. People unconsciously give signs that you can learn to "read." Having mastered this alphabet, it is much easier to see the true attitude towards yourself.

Folk rumor

Judging a person by someone else's words is an ungrateful affair; perhaps he is not at all what his neighbors, a former boss, or his wife say he is. They may have their selfish interests associated with the intentional desire to harm. But if you hear negative things about him from many people, you should be more careful. For comparison, we can give the rating of sellers on a large trading platform. If you see a particular seller having low ratings from different buyers, acquiring something from him will be very risky. Do not risk in vain.

Professional trickster

Each fraudster has his narrow specialization, and therefore they know the psychology of their victims very well. Many dodgers use the desire of women to get married as soon as possible. If you are in an active search, have a good salary, but at the same time there is little chance of a good party, you can get into the view of such a person. The first time with him will be like a fairy tale: a guy in love sings serenades to you, communication with him makes your heart tremble. But suddenly he will "happen" a great misfortune, which urgently needs money. As soon as he receives what he wants from you, he will disappear forever. Therefore, be vigilant and do not succumb to the affectionate speeches of someone who wants to use you. A man who is aimed at a serious relationship, won't ask for money from a new acquaintance, but on the contrary, will do everything to be considered self-sufficient.

Lonely women also often fall into the network of married men, spending their whole lives in the expectation that he is about to divorce. And after all, they know that their chances of moving from simple flirting to real relationships are negligible, but they still hope that in their case, there will be an exception to the rule.

"Another's soul is darkness," says folk wisdom. The way it is. Unless, of course, you have special knowledge and skills. Have you ever wondered how clairvoyants "work"? Among them are talents who have developed what nature has given them. But most of all, seers hone a couple of techniques to help them in their work. And that's all. And then—a matter of practice and experience.

In this section, we begin to come close to some professional secrets of communication success. Moreover, in any place, at any time, in any state, etc. And all people know how to do it, but they do it subconsciously, i.e., without fully realizing how they succeed in communicating, acting, and opposing other people's influence so successfully. As a rule, each of us subconsciously owns a couple of three techniques at the amateur level—this is a kind of our survival strategy in this world. But, since even gifted people do not train and develop their skills, they also remain amateurs, like us.

You can master dozens of effective techniques. And if you constantly pay due attention to them, then you will get everything you want in this life. This is how all famous people act. The line is yours.

Face, pose and gestures

The first indicator of a person's psyche is his face, or rather his facial expression. Indeed, a villain may be hiding behind a beautiful face, and a decent and kind person may turn out to be terrible. Therefore, everything becomes clear when a person comes to life—according to his facial expressions.

Another indicator is a person's posture. If you are told about compassion, and with their whole appearance, they show indifference, then everything becomes clear to you without explanation. Gait, as a pose in motion, also very clearly characterizes the state of a person.

Most often, the process of communication is accompanied by gestures, which are also very informative. With the help of gestures, we try to convey our message more accurately and, accordingly, we perceive it more accurately.

Now, watching your interlocutor, pay attention to how his facial expressions, posture, and gestures coincide with what he tells you. How much you will discover for yourself! And this is just the beginning.

Ask questions

It is very useful to ask questions, since it is very easy for an inexperienced person to deceive himself in other people's words, not to mention other people's manipulations. This happens for several reasons, one of which is the difference in the perception of the world. Yes, we are all human, but we perceive the world differently. It turns out that we find in our interlocutor's words our meaning, which is very far from that which the interlocutor puts into his words. From here, quarrels and disagreements and similar troubles begin. It is worth noting that there are times when we understand each other perfectly.

But this is a separate conversation

If you ask questions, especially in those cases when you are not completely sure of the correct understanding of some meanings in the words of the interlocutor, then you can find a lot of interesting things about your perception, correct it and avoid unnecessary quarrels.

Do not wander in the clouds

There are no miracles in the world—in the right sense of this expression in this context. Develop sober thinking. Romance is romance, but some things and events are not even described in fairy tales. And people so willingly believe everything and anything... And why? Partly from low literacy, partly from little experience, partly from naivety, and partly from an unwillingness to sometimes think critically.

What are they telling you?

Voice is one of the individual characteristics of every living creature.

Watch what you are told. It may not be stupidity and not fairy tales, but quite real things, only little relevant. Such things are said to obscure your consciousness and further inspire you with some truths. Being not quite attentive to the words of the interlocutor, we can skip very important information, and without giving it any importance, promise something, putting ourselves in a very difficult position. And you never know...

As they say to you

In addition to what they tell you, pay attention to how you are told. The effect is the same as when watching facial expressions and gestures. Intonation must strictly correspond to the meaning. If someone tells you that he loves you, his intonation will be congruent with the words of love, and at the same time, it will have nothing to do with the intonation that accompanies the words of hatred and contempt.

Do not forget that not only you can master this skill...

CHAPTER 5

HOW TO DISCOVER DARK PEOPLE'S MASKS

Many people are successful, happy, or seem to have perfect lives. But is this the case? Not always, as many of them pretend. This is called wearing a mask.

These are depressed people who are optimistic, anxious people who seem relaxed, and people who choose to wear a mask so that others do not see what they are.

Do you want to know the different masks we wear and their reasons? We will explain everything in this chapter!

The controller

A person who controls all aspects of his life may have been betrayed before. Faced with this pain, the person develops a behavior that will allow him to ensure that others keep their promise. Thus, he will avoid being betrayed again.

The controller hides feelings of insecurity. Thus, it is essential to control everything and even sometimes in an exaggerated way.

The mask protects him from the pain of another betrayal, while he tries to do everything to prevent it from happening again.

The rigid

A rigid person has suffered great injustices before. Faced with this, he/she becomes inflexible, constantly seeking justice and the accuracy of things.

A rigid person becomes a perfectionist, to the point that it turns into an obsession. Everything must be in place!

Thus, studying everything perfectly will prevent injustice from ringing at our door. This is why the rigid act this way.

The addict

A dependent person often carries the pain of feeling abandoned. This injury generates indifference towards others, so as not to feel abandoned again. This avoids taking any relationship seriously while rejecting the idea of living with someone.

The pain of abandonment is terrible. The addicted person suffers from the depths of his or her being unable to depend on someone or failing to believe that the people who are important to them will never abandon them.

The leaker

The person fleeing rejects company. She prefers solitude and moments of calm. She rejects being the center of attention because it scares her.

A person who is fleeing behaves like this because he has been rejected and because it causes such an injury in him that he prefers to avoid it.

Leaky people cannot bear not knowing how to act in certain situations, being ashamed or feeling lost, simply because it would cause a rejection on the part of others.

In their solitude, they are neither vulnerable nor uncertain. Their mask protects them from what makes them suffer. Would it be cowardice? No! It is simply a matter of preventing what we cannot control from hurting ourselves.

The masochist

It may be a mental or emotional masochist. This attitude is due to a feeling of humiliation and shame dating from a past situation.

This then provokes this masochistic attitude, always pushing to want to solve the problems of others by all means, regardless of whether one is humiliated or belittled.

The masochist does not act like the profiles we saw just before, and he does not try to avoid or flee his injuries.

The masochist faces what hurts him, sometimes seeking to suffer even more. He was hurt, and he had no control.

Today he is in control, and it is he who decides who will harm him or not. Deep down, it helps him to overcome the situation.

We were able to see that there are several different and varied masks, which are most often explained by a past emotional injury.

Do you recognize someone in these different profiles? It is easy to identify people who wear a mask, as they sometimes leave their true personality hidden.

It is best to overcome what causes this fear in us. Perhaps the masochist is hard on himself, but he at least faces his pain.

This can make him stronger and allow him to overcome his trauma, or, on the contrary, make himself suffer even more.

And you, what do you think of all this? What is your point of view?

CHAPTER 6

THE POKER FACE MYTHS

We have all put on a poker face sometimes even without knowing it, especially children during interrogation after some mischief. Consciously or unconsciously, we all use body expression and our gestures, voluntarily or not, to convey a message. The body speaks, and that is why in some cases, we have to make it shut up, especially if you are Patrick Antonius or if you are in a poker game where you do not want anyone to know your emotions. But this board game is not exclusive to putting a poker face, and although its use has become more popular, especially since the appearance in 2010 of the 4chan forum, putting a poker face has been used throughout history both in the gaming world as in politics, associated with well-known characters like Trump or Putin or even in anthropological studies.

An important reference is found in the British writer Henry Jones' book "Round Games at Cards, "published in 1875, who describes " Poker face " as the expression we adopt when we do not want to transmit anything. What we would rather call an expressionless state.

In 1934, the novelist Graham Greene wrote a critique of Sir Arthur Conan Doyle, titled "The Poker Face," referring to his outstanding work in his novel Sherlock Homes. Here the detective and the author worked the same concept showing that who controls the true poker face, in the end, will learn how to read the opponent's face. María Konnikova, a Russian-American psychologist who published an essay called "How to Think Like Sherlock Holmes," would also write about this character.

There are different types of research such as "The Poker Face of Wall Street" by Aaron Brown, where the relationship between the world of finance and the gaming system in poker is analyzed, or "Poker Faces" by David Hayano. He published his anthropological study based on the impenetrable face of poker players. Or in the artistic field like the series of photographs "Poker Face" by Ulvis Albert about the WSOP published in 1981.

Many examples of the use of the poker face as part of an emotional control strategy can also be found in sports. Grantland Rice described Helen Wills, Winner of 19 Grand Slam titles in the 1920s, including "Little Miss Poker Face."

It was precisely tennis and science that demonstrated a few years ago that our actions are evident not just on the lips, but also on our body or our movements,

43

voluntary or not. Israeli Hillel Aviezer conducted this study as a result of a collaboration between Princeton and Jerusalem universities; it was carried out through an investigation into the expressions of Serena Williams and Rafa Nadal during moments of great tension that would be shared by photographs with 45 students. These, divided into groups, would have access either to different parts of the body, to the complete photograph, or only to the face. The result confirmed that the mind deceives us more commonly than we think and that joy and sadness are best seen in our hands, arms, legs, and even veins.

In the poker world, in addition to the necessary sunglasses, some prefer to play with a good long-necked sweater to conceal any traitorous veins that swell in us because of the stress of the table or with a cap that covers our ears. As useful information, we recommend gloves for your kit if you are one of those who sweat from the nerves or those who bite their nails.

Now you know that putting on a poker face helps but it is not everything. You must also learn to control certain unconscious movements that can give you away. Of course, do not pretend to become a mime, the strategy is important but knowing how to play is even more so.

CHAPTER 7

HOW TO UNDERSTAND AN HONEST EMOTION VS. FAKE AND MANIPULATED EMOTIONS

It seems very simple to say, and the reality is that simple: you feel good when you solve your problems easily. Without drama, you are full of energy and vitality, you feel optimistic...that is when you are using authentic emotions.

An emotion is authentic when it responds to the stimulus that mobilizes it. This demolishes the terms "positive emotion" and "negative emotion" that have become obsolete when verifying that all emotions are necessary, and that fear or anger should not always be negative.

And what stimulus mobilizes an emotion so that it is authentic?

First of all, I have to say that each emotion must come into operation with a single stimulus. In this way, we will obtain the benefits of each one, and we will be able to verify that all the emotions if used well, are fundamental for a life of well-being:

FEAR: response to the THREAT stimulus, and its objective is to set limits to any invasion or danger to obtain SECURITY. Ana was upset that her best friend called her at any time regardless of her privacy; she began to feel angry and criticize her behind her back. Anger, in this case, would be a false emotion because the stimulus is threatening; with authentic fear, she would set limits asking for respect, and she would feel safer.

SADNESS: response to the stimulus of LOSS, and its objective is to think to solve and thus learn and DEVELOP. José left his partner; he was afraid of being alone and not finding another love story as beautiful as the one he lived. This had him distressed. Fear was a false emotion because what he suffered was a loss, not a threat. With sadness, he would accept and look for ways to improve from experience.

ANGER: response to the encouragement of LIE (manipulation, abuse, treason, injustice), and its objective is to take action to react and cut through deception to do JUSTICE. Eva suffered the betrayal of a colleague in her own business, and she felt sad because she did not expect such an outcome, so she felt guilty and did not raise her head. Sadness was a false emotion because we are talking about treason. With rage, she would have expressed herself and would have cut off the traitor, thus bringing justice to her life.

PRIDE: response to the encouragement of ADMIRATION, and its objective is to dare to value greatness in others and oneself, avoiding comparisons, its purpose is RECOGNITION. Silvia was invited to participate in a Congress with a presentation, she began to feel fear, and this led her to feel inferior to the other speakers. Fear was a false emotion that weakened her. The right thing would have been to feel pride for the other speakers and also for herself, who had the opportunity to take a brave step towards her dreams.

LOVE: response to the stimulus SAFE SPACE and its objective is the dedication to everything worthwhile to achieve BELONGING with whomever one chooses. Marta dedicated herself to "saving" all the people she saw in need and then complained bitterly that she did not receive even a small part of what she gave. Here the false emotion is love because giving someone who only wants to take advantage of it is a threat, not a safe space. The authentic emotion would be to feel afraid and to set limits when it comes to delivery.

JOY: response to the stimulus of UNEXPECTED GIFT, and its objective is to open up opportunities and flow with life in freedom to feel FULL. Manuel was a little curmudgeon, and it bothered him that his wife went to yoga and then stayed to have a beer with her friends. He saw it as something unfair while he was bored alone at home. He felt false anger. The real thing would have been to connect with the joy of enjoyment and seek something pleasurable for him instead of angering the joy of others.

With these examples, you can see that all emotions can be very damaging when used to face the wrong stimulus. For this reason, there are no positive or negative emotions, but authentic or false, that is, adequate or inadequately used. It is just a matter of re-learning their language, being alert to the stimulus, and using the correct emotion in each case.

A false emotion is ALWAYS accompanied by discomfort, negative energy, lack of vitality and enthusiasm, problems that accumulate one after another, anxiety, and stress. Also included are other somatizations that produce emotional dysfunctions caused by the use of emotions that do not respond to your stimulus.

Envy, resentment, feelings of guilt, interesting relationships, dependency, impotence, the feeling of inferiority, or superiority. All these are dysfunctions that are produced by using false emotions.

If you want your life to prosper, you have no choice but to manage your emotions. Otherwise, it will be them who will direct your life, and you will be doomed to suffer one disaster after another.

CHAPTER 8

WHEN THE LIE HITS HOME

If falsely attributing yourself to fantastic situations or characteristics turns into a compulsion, it may be a sign that there is a personality disorder that hides suffering.

The "Pinocchio syndrome," also known by the name of "pathological liar," and with the name of "mythomania," is the one suffered by those who lie consciously and compulsively to obtain a benefit.

The pathological liar lies intending to hide something that he does not accept from his story. His lies are spontaneous and unplanned, and, once embedded in this dynamic of farce and deceit, he cannot stop, which is why he maintains his deceits on many occasions for years. The pathological liar knows he is lying, but he cannot help it until he finally ends up believing his fables.

Mythomania is defined as a tendency to lie or to tell fabulous things. For the sole purpose of not engaging in naïveté, we must recognize that lying is very frequent, social, and universal behavior, both to justify behaviors and not to make others suffer. It is a common resource to hide something, so as not to hurt or harm. However, there is a type of lie that we would call "pathological" that afflicts people who invent great realities and that have nothing to do with their lives. It is the one enunciated by those who disfigure or disguise situations in their personal, economic, social, or work life. They are not people whose behavior can be seen, because they do not look like unbalanced people, so it is very easy to fall into their deceptions. However, like all complexes, it has its roots in childhood, when self-esteem has had early failures. One of the possible causes is that the parents did not value their qualities or compared them with siblings or cousins; and, later, with the companions. The mythomaniac, as a compensation mechanism for his battered and devalued narcissism, invents, and fantasizes about situations to level himself out before others.

Of course, only very insecure people present this tendency and this psychic work of omitting, lying, exaggerating, and falsifying reality to try to be accepted.

Origins

This disorder can be due to different reasons, namely:

—It may be that the mythomaniac belongs to a family

that lives on social simulation, on appearance, showing what they do not have and what they are not.

–It may be that his life is so intolerable concerning the ideals and fantasies that he or his family deposited in him that by not being able to satisfy them, instead of accepting the truth, he takes the path of "inventing" another reality that only exists in his head.

One of the most notable characteristics of mythomaniacs is low self-esteem, given their non-acceptance of themselves and the deep and impossible desire to be another. And the devaluation is so great that they have to appeal to anything to be admired and accepted by people.

Coexistence

In coexistence, whether family or work, with the mythomaniac, their situation becomes more difficult, since others begin to suspect and gradually discover that their word is not worth believing. The feeling it generates for who received the effects of mythomania is to feel mocked, deceived. Those who make up their environment feel that they do not know who he is or what he wants and, thus, colleagues, friends, and even family members are taking distance. Consequently, the mythomaniac is often left very alone.

Of course, it is quite complicated to live with these people. First, because they are usually very trained and used to handling. They are always pretending, cheating, omitting, inventing things from the smallest to situations that can lead to serious consequences. And because they are compelling, people tend to believe them at first.

They can even take risky attitudes, like stealing or spreading rumors in offices for the sole purpose of harming someone. Because, by not accepting any mistake they may have made, they may end up awarding it to a partner. And, since, of course, they are not willing to recognize their lies, by force of repeating them, they end up believing them. Hence it is quite difficult for them to consult their own with a mental health specialist; it is rather the family, worried, desperate, who asks for help. When this happens, one of the recommendations made is to confront the compulsive liar or mythomaniac, with his long lists of deceits and omissions. In the first place, so that the compulsion to lie does not continue to grow and also because, although it is an emotional disorder in their personality, they are not crazy. And deep down they know perfectly well that they have a problem and that alone they cannot get out of it.

Compulsion

The mythomaniac cannot stop lying and, precisely for this reason, his is a true compulsion.

He does not tell a lie to cover himself or justify himself as any person can eventually do, but he does it always and does not measure the harmful consequences that it can cause.

In general terms, this condition is the expression of an alteration in the construction of the personality that leads the person to thin their ties systematically and to ensure that nobody believes anything.

Being a mythomaniac has negative consequences; the person who lies compulsively loses credibility and social prestige.

It is often said of them: "Don't believe him because he is a charlatan."

Nuances

"Whoever told the first lie founded the civil society," said Irish playwright and novelist Oscar Wilde.

On some occasions, the lie arises as a necessity, in the face of a possible real or fantasized threat of losing our place, our prestige, our romantic relationship. In these cases, we can think of lying as a defense mechanism against the anguish of loss, and this characteristic makes it universal, without respecting creeds, ages, and relationships.

Lying comes from the Latin word "mens" (mind). Lying well means intelligence to have full knowledge of the truth; it also means understanding what the other wants to hear or, better said, entering the mind of the person who will listen to the lie, which makes it a creative fact.

Fear is a great cause of deception, but some lies are widely accepted by society, those that are linked to the promotion of products, services, people, candidates. In this case, qualities are exaggerated, and possible failures or defects are omitted.

Socially, the lie that avoids pain or suffering is also admitted and promoted. So the nuances between the collectively accepted and rejected forms require a certain skill acquired with induction or upbringing.

In the mythomaniac, the behavior of falsifying reality, deceiving (in some cases it includes defamation or accusations against people), took root in the personality.

These people live in a state of permanent anxiety because they have reached extreme behavior, and to stop making lies is difficult, so it is a compulsion.

CHAPTER 9

THE POWER OF EMOTIONAL INTELLIGENCE

The ability to read people can also be used for the dark side of emotional intelligence.

In some jobs, the connection with emotions is essential, while in others, it is harmful. Like any skill, the ability to read people can be used for good and evil. Some of the greatest events in human history have been triggered by emotional intelligence.

When Martin Luther King, Jr. set out his dream, he chose words that would move the hearts of his audience. Instead of respecting the sacred obligation of freedom, King said, America gave blacks an uncovered check.

He believed that a country suffocated by the heat of oppression could be turned into an oasis of freedom and justice. So he predicted a future in which the sons of former slaves and sons of former slave owners could sit together for a hundred fraternities on the red hills of Georgia.

Communicating such an exciting message required emotional intelligence—the ability to recognize, understand, and manage emotions. Dr. King demonstrated extraordinary ability in managing his emotions and in awakening the emotions that propelled his audience to action.

As the writer of his speeches, Clarence Jones said, King conveyed a perfectly balanced protest of reason and emotion, anger, and hope. His tone of painful indignation was completely in line with that.

What is Emotional Intelligence?

Although numerous authors have contributed to the definition of emotional intelligence, certainly, the most important is Daniel Goleman, because of which the term EI became known to the whole world. He published his first book in 1995, while his later editions were limited to establishing the existence of EI. Goleman later extended his work on EI to the field of leadership and linked EI to performance in the workplace.

Today there are several models and theories of EI. One of the definitions was given by Meyer and Saloway, who introduced the term EI into psychology:

- Emotional intelligence is the capacity to interpret emotions, analyze and produce them to help us understand emotions and emotional awareness and to control emotions to reflexively encourage emotional and mental development.

- Another definition of Mayer and Nightingale, which is also generally known, is: Emotional intelligence is a type of social intelligence that includes the ability to track the thoughts and emotions of one's own and of others, discriminate against them, and use that knowledge to understand others' opinions and behavior. Emotional Intelligence (Salovey & Mayer, 1990).

Models of emotional intelligence

There are three different EI models, which differ depending on the definition and operationalization of the term. Thus, there is an ability model, a mixed model, and a line model, and we will briefly look at each of them.

1) The creators of the first model, the ability model, are Saloway and Mayer, who consider EI based on four components:

- Accurate identification of emotions ("How do I feel?"),
- Using emotions as an aid in thinking ("What effect do emotions have on me?"),

- Understanding the effects (consequences) of emotions ("What is the cause of these emotions?"),
- Managing emotions to make good choices and focus on effective action ("How do I manage these emotions?").

2) Daniel Goleman is the creator of the so-called mixed model, which includes five components:

- Self-awareness (the ability to recognize emotions when they are manifested, recognizing the impact they have on other people, is essential for psychological self-knowledge and self-understanding, the inability to recognize our emotions leads us to depend on them),
- Self-regulation (overcoming and managing emotions, adapting to new situations, people who are better at self-regulation recover faster than life falls),
- Social skills (the ability to maintain relationships with others that largely depends on the skill of understanding other people's emotions),
- Empathy (respecting the feelings of other people, more empathetic people can better interpret existing social signals),

- Motivation (what drives us to succeed and for the sake of achievement).

Goleman adds, in addition to these five components, a set of emotional competencies that are within each of these five components. Emotional competencies are not innate, but are acquired through experience and can be developed. Furthermore, Goleman states that there is a general EI with which people are born that determines their potential to learn certain competencies.

3) The third type of model is based on the assumption that EI can be viewed as a set of personality traits, and Constantine Vasili Petrides gave the setting of the model. This model defines EI as a constellation of emotional self-perception that is located at lower levels in the personality hierarchy. Thus, EI is considered as a self-perception of emotional abilities, and another name given to this model is " emotional self-efficacy based on traits. "

There are numerous findings that emotions are sometimes more important and that the rational part of the mind prevails. Various studies involving injuries to regions responsible for emotional data processing indicate that emotional intelligence is different from general intelligence.

In addition to numerous criticisms, EI has managed to find its purpose, and today it is used in many global companies to determine leadership skills, to predict violence among young people, to determine the links between emotions and prosocial behavior and the like. Although EI is challenged in terms of prediction of behavior, it justifies a significant impact when it comes to the use of psychoactive substances (which negatively correlates with EI), self-confidence (the higher the score on the EI test, the higher the level of self-confidence), business, i.e., work performance (high positive association with EI) and related areas of human behavior.

Hallmarks of the Emotional Mind

The study of emotional intelligence takes its official beginning in 1937 when approaching our topic. Hereditary psychologist, a student of his father, Robert Thorndike, published work on social intelligence of the same name. In 1940, the outstanding psychologist David Wexler (also a former student of Thorndike's father) opened the next stage with an article on intellectual and non-intellectual components. He pointed out that non-intellectual components are even more important for social adaptation than intellectual ones. It was with them that a serious study of this phenomenon began. An important milestone was also 1983 when Howard Gardner wrote about multiple intelligence and 1990 when American psychologists John Meyer and Peter Salovey introduced the term "emotional intelligence" and began a research program to measure it. We'll mention Daniel Goleman's book "Emotional Intelligence," which was published in 1995 and has become classic: even though the term itself is not his idea.

We owe Meyer and Saloway the definition of emotional intelligence. Scientists described it based on its constituent parts.

Emotional intelligence is a combination of four skills, among which:

- The accuracy of evaluating and expressing emotions is the ability to determine emotions according to their physical state and thoughts, appearance, and behavior. This also includes the ability to express your emotions and related needs to other people;
- The use of emotions in mental activity is an understanding of how you can think more effectively using emotions. Many human problems come from the fact that one does not know how to control his emotions, does not understand them, and is not able to

control them. If he has such a skill, he gains an invaluable gift—the ability to stand in the other's position, look at himself from the side, and evaluate the situation from different points of view. All this is the ability to see the world from different angles. This skill is extremely productive because it allows you to regulate relationships and find solutions to pressing problems;

- Understanding emotions is the ability to determine the source of emotions, classify them, and recognize the relationship between words and emotions. It is also the ability to interpret the meanings of emotions related to relationships, understand complex feelings, and be aware of transitions from one emotion to another. Researchers include here the possible further development of emotion;
- Managing emotions is the ability to use the information that they give, evoke emotions or move away from them, depending on their information content or usefulness; manage your own and others' emotions.

Emotional intelligence, fortunately, can be developed. This is not what is given to us from birth and for life. Although, for example, J. Meyer believes that it is impossible to increase the level of emotional intelligence, because, in his opinion, this is just a given. And then he admits that through training, you can increase the level of emotional competence—the ability to recognize your feelings and feelings of other people with the goals of self-motivation and control your emotions.

Among his opponents, we see a very authoritative D. Goleman, a true titan in the study of emotional intelligence. Goleman believes that emotional intelligence can be developed because the nerve pathways of the brain continue to develop until the middle of human life. The methods for developing emotional intelligence can be very different. Among them, everyone will find at least one that is most suitable: family education, relationships in society, close relationships with the opposite sex, and simply life experience itself, which, as you know, is the best teacher.

When studies of emotional intelligence became widely available, they turned out to be the missing link in a specific question: why do people with average intelligence (IQ) seventy percent of the time outperform competitors with the highest intelligence? This problem cast a dense shadow on what people have always mistaken for the only source of success: intelligence. Decades of research now point to the emotional component of intelligence as a decisive factor.

Emotional intelligence consists of four basic skills that describe personal and social competence.

Personal competence consists of our self-awareness and self-management skills, which focus more on us individually than on our interactions with other people. Personal competence is the ability of a person to be aware of his emotions and control his behavior and inclinations. Two skills belong to it:

Self-awareness - the ability to accurately feel your own emotions and track their appearance and development. We are aware of our own emotions, the way they affect our thoughts and behavior, we know our strengths and weaknesses, and maintain self-confidence;

Self-government - the ability to use an understanding of one's emotions to remain flexible and positively direct one's behavior. We can manage impulsive feelings and actions, manage our emotions (in healthy ways!), take the initiative, fulfill obligations, and adapt to changing circumstances.

Social competence consists of understanding the processes taking place in our environment and of relationship management skills. Social competence is our ability to understand the mood of other people, their behavior and motives, to improve the quality of our relationships. This also includes two skills:

Social understanding - the ability to accurately notice the emotions of other people and understand what is happening. Thanks to this skill, we can understand the emotions, needs, and problems of others, and feel comfortable in society;

Relationship management - the ability to use an understanding of one's and other's emotions to manage interactions with other people successfully. We know how to develop and maintain good relationships, how to communicate, inspire others, how to work well in a team and find a way out of conflict situations.

Emotional intelligence, IQ, and personality are two different things. Emotional intelligence is a fundamental element of human behavior that is distinct from intelligence. There is no known connection between a measure of intelligence and emotional intelligence; it is completely impossible to predict the level of emotional intelligence based on how smart someone is, that is, how high his IQ is. IQ itself is misunderstood as a degree of education or as an indicator of genius. IQ in itself is your ability to learn, and at fifteen, you have the same as at fifty. Emotional intelligence is a versatile collection of skills which can be theoretically learned and developed. Although some people naturally have higher emotional intelligence than others, if you wish, you can develop emotional intelligence to a high level, even if you were not born with it.

Individuality is the last piece of the mosaic. It is a sustainable style that defines each of us. Individuality is the result of deep preferences, such as a tendency to focus on oneself or, conversely, to extrovert behavior. However, like IQ, personality cannot be used to predict the level of emotional intelligence. Like IQ, personality is stable and does not change throughout life. IQ, emotional intelligence, and individuality—each of these phenomena represent a unique basis for the interaction of a person with himself and with the world around him.

Emotional intelligence affects:

Our success at work. Emotional intelligence helps to manage contacts, which especially important if a person is working in a team or if his work is related to communication (and the vast majority of classes are suitable for these criteria). EQ helps motivate people, and if there is an element of competition in work, surpass rivals. Communicating with the heads of the personnel services of large companies, you can find out that, when selecting for a job, they consider EQ the same as professional skills, and often require an EQ test before accepting a candidate;

Physical health. Modern life is stressful, and it is a fact. Of course, some people have less stress, but in general, it is not about who has more, who has less, but how much a person can manage it. If you are unable to control the level of stress, this can lead to serious health problems. No wonder they say all the diseases come from the nerves: excessive stress may raise blood pressure, weaken the immune system, raise the risk of a heart attack, lead to infertility, and accelerate the aging process. Therefore, the first step to improving emotional intelligence is to try to learn and understand how to reduce stress;

Mental Health. Uncontrolled stress can also affect a person's mental health, making them vulnerable to anxiety and depression. Unable to manage our emotions, we find ourselves subject to mood changes, and the inability to control ourselves leads to the inability to form strong relationships, which in the end can make us acutely experience loneliness;

Relationship. Understanding our emotions and knowing how to manage them, we can better express our feelings and understand what other people feel and how. This skill allows us to communicate more efficiently and create stronger relationships both at work and in personal life.

So, emotional intelligence is associated with success at work. Think about how much your emotional intelligence affects professional success. Short answer: very strongly! Because it is a powerful way to focus energy in one direction with a huge result. Social psychologists from the Aristotle University of Greece, future candidates of science, during a large-scale study, comparing emotional intelligence with thirty-three other skills important for work, found that it was emotional intelligence that is the strongest predictor of success at work. It determines fifty-eight percent of success, and in all professional areas. Fifty-eight percent—think, it's more than half! And it turns out that such important factors as IQ, profile education, previous experience, etc. account for even less than half of the merits!

Our emotional intelligence is the basis for acquiring critical skills. It affects most of what we say and do every day. Emotional intelligence is the most important criterion for success in the workplace. For those who aim at a high position, this is the most important factor in leadership and personal superiority.

Among the study participants were executives, including large international companies; it turned out that ninety percent of them have a very high level of emotional intelligence. At the same time, only twenty percent of employees holding grassroots positions have a highly developed emotional intelligence, which means that sooner or later, they will occupy a much higher position. If others develop their emotional intelligence, their capabilities will also improve markedly. You can be the main person in the company without emotional intelligence, but the chances are small.

People with a high degree of emotional intelligence obviously gain more money than people with low EQ. The relationship between emotional intelligence and income is so direct that each point in emotional intelligence adds two percent to the annual salary. Of course, two percent is not much, but this is for each point! The data obtained is stored for employees in all industries, at all levels, in every region of the world. So far, experts have not found a field of activity in which success and salary would not be closely related to emotional intelligence.

Emotional intelligence can be developed. This is certainly his most encouraging property. The actual basis of emotional intelligence is the link between our emotional and logical "brains." The pathway to emotional intelligence begins in the brain; when an event occurs with us, our primary feelings emerge here and through the limbic system breakthrough to the forefront of the brain before we can think rationally about what happened. And, before the mind can comprehend them, we have an emotional response to events. Therefore, emotional intelligence requires good communication between the brain's logical and emotional centers.

There is such a term - "plasticity." Neurologists use it to describe the brain's ability to change. The brain grows new connections while we learn new skills. Changes are gradual and occur because brain cells develop new connections to accelerate the effectiveness of newly acquired skills. Using strategies for developing emotional intelligence allows billions of microscopic neurons that pave the road between the rational and emotional centers of the brain to "pull branches" to reach other cells. One cell can grow fifteen thousand bonds with neighbors. When we train our brains constantly using new strategies of emotional intelligence, emotionally intelligent behavior becomes a habit.

Busting The Myths About Emotional Intelligence

Many people tell that they cannot develop this Emotional Intelligence "business" because they are very nervous; others say that they have tried several times and were unsuccessful. Some say that they have tried to like everyone around them and have not succeeded.

The three great myths about emotional intelligence:

1 - You won't be nervous anymore, or you won't be angry anymore: Lie!

Emotional Intelligence does not lie in failing to feel what is natural for us human beings to feel in different situations in our lives, such as anger, hurt, sadness, disappointment. What changes with Emotional Intelligence is that you will start to notice that you feel a certain way and will start to measure your words and attitudes. For example, instead of yelling at that annoying coworker who keeps disturbing your performance, you may even feel irritated in the same way, but you will be able to consider the best attitude to solve the problem. Not just to vent the irritation that caused you.

It is important to know that having Emotional Intelligence does not mean becoming a cold person.

Without feelings, quite the contrary, you will be even more connected with your emotions. However, aware of what you are feeling and how each emotion influences your attitudes, you will refine your reactions, stop acting on the emotional impulse, and act in an increasingly balanced and effective way.

2 - Understanding what Emotional Intelligence means will make you balanced: Lie!

It is not enough to read all the literature that exists about EI and think that this will be enough to become an emotionally balanced person. Your emotions cannot be mapped, understood, and managed overnight, and this is a job for every day of your life. You will always be learning new things about yourself, even because we are beings of constant change. What makes you feel good today, may be what hurts you tomorrow and vice-versa. If you wait for a magic book, a magical consultation with a renowned psychologist, or even with a miraculous guru to achieve emotional balance overnight, I'm sorry, but I need to ask you to "take the horse out of the rain."

Dedicate yourself to self-knowledge and never give up on being a better person, be patient with yourself, and seek learning in each of your mistakes. Think of it as a journey of a thousand steps where each small step brings you closer to a lighter and more successful life.

3 - You will like everyone around you: Not even close!

When talking about balanced people who get along with everyone, there is a great tendency to interpret that these people like everyone and that everyone likes them. That does not exist! There will always be that person that your "saint" just doesn't hit or even that person who doesn't like you no matter how well you treat them. EI only contributes so that you can get along with all these people and get along well!

Imagine that coworker who keeps talking bad about you to the whole office and the worst, in front of you still pretends to be your friend. It's bad to have to look at him every day, isn't it? A lot of people just can't even look, talk then becomes impossible. However, EI allows you to separate the chaff from the wheat and still create an environment of light coexistence with everyone, opening the door to good communication and, in the vast majority of cases converting boring colleagues into great work partners.

Just respect that no one is obliged to like you and vice versa, but in 99% of the cases, it is possible to maintain coexistence on a light and productive level. But if you want that, you will have to start from yourself, whoever waits for others is always living according to what they have to offer when you could offer something much better to yourself and the world.

Many demand that the world is a better place, but few are those who exchange posters for attitudes!

CHAPTER 10

SCHOOLING THE EMOTIONS

Educate emotions for what? Development of emotional intelligence, emotional competence, awareness of our emotions, quality of life.

Many people still don't understand the importance of developing emotional intelligence. A survey shows that in the last 30 years of the last century in the USA, 87% of people who lost their jobs lost them due to difficulties related to the lack of good use of emotional intelligence. The consequences of the lack of emotional education, just citing the data collected in developed countries, according to Claude Steiner, include delinquency, increased abuse of licit and illicit drugs, traffic accidents and conflicts. Also included are violence at all levels and social sectors, homicides and suicides, physical and sexual abuse of women and children, abandoned children, and unemployment at all levels. Further, conduct problems and dropping out of childhood and adolescence in all social classes, marital problems, separations, conflicts between parents and children, depression and psychosomatic illnesses were noted. It is easy to see that these situations happen precisely because of the lack of emotional intelligence development.

Emotional competence is an essential component of personal power. By making our relationships stimulating and mutually rewarding, we feel encouraged, optimistic, and powerful. It enables any dialogue, human contact, or association to provide greater rewards to all involved. Good communication makes it possible to confirm perceptions, give and receive feedback effectively, and honesty of feelings are essential elements for a person to live in balance.

Emotional competence is made up of the ability to get to know each other, understand emotions and feelings, and expressing them productively. It also involves having self-control and empathy with other people, and thus understanding what they feel and interacting with them. Being emotionally competent is being able to deal with emotions in order to develop your personal power and the quality of life that surrounds you.

When we educate our emotions, our relationships expand. We create the possibility of affection between people, cooperative work becomes more viable, and the sense of community is facilitated. Many people, especially men, imagine that emotional education will result in a loss of power in their personal and professional lives. But the truth is that we all have something to learn from our emotions.

As we learn to read and write, we can develop the ability to deal with our emotions and feelings, and for this, there are a series of simple methodologies and techniques that allow this development at any age. The development of emotions begins with the awareness of our emotions and feelings, a differentiation between them, and learning to name each of them. It also involves understanding where they come from and how they work, learning to talk about what we feel, overcoming fear and inhibitions, and directing them positively. As we do this, natural empathy and intelligent interaction with other people develop, and we develop relationship skills. Naturally, the levels of stress and anxiety go down, and we can live with more joy, health, and quality.

What Is Emotion?

Emotion is a response from our body to an external stimulus. The relationships with others or the events that surround us cause an impact, which is translated into some kind of emotion.

The emotion we feel, for example, the sadness after receiving bad news, has physiological consequences such as a shaky voice, the pallor on the face, or the change in gestures. On the other hand, there are psychological consequences, that is, the feelings that remain as a result of some emotion.

Why Do We Need Emotions?

The human being is the most evolved being by nature. This being has a body that comprises exclusively animal parts and exclusively human parts. Almost every organ in the human body is anatomically analogous to that of other animals in its class. Although some animals have some organs with greater capacities than humans, they have a developed anatomical set that surpasses all the capabilities of all others.

Result of thousands and thousands of years of natural evolution, the human vocal apparatus that produces dozens of phonemes and its brain that memorizes them, formed the ideal duo for the creation of rationality. Speak and think, and memorize what you think and say, only man can do it.

Human rationalization has created new values, new ideas, and new realities. And these new realities have reinforced the growth of others. The language has forced the development of the brain and vice versa, and both forced to the development of the entire human body. The human senses have become the most developed - the refining of taste, smell, hearing, and especially touch, is very developed in man, as well as vision, namely in their sensitivity to colors.

All of these aspects create new needs for human beings, including ways of expressing themselves, not only what they felt for their animal nature, but also for what they felt for their capacity for mental creation. For this reason, nature has endowed human beings with unique characteristics, such as the ability to blush because they lie, cry because they are sad or laugh because they are happy.

Any emotional feeling is an accumulation of tension that comes from everything around us, or from ourselves, and goes against our ability to react or to understand immediately. Emotions are the way to defuse that tension.

Animals have no understanding, so they have no feelings, so they do not accumulate emotional or nervous tension, and therefore they do not laugh or cry.

If a person wants to do something but does not do it because conscience—society, culture, religion, the law and everything that is of human origin—do not allow it, then a certain emotional tension will be created that it can be expressed in the most varied ways: with depression, violence, apathy, and usually accompanied with sadness because it is a negative tension. In the same way, if a person is calmed by something he did not expect, or feels a satisfaction greater than imagined, he is also unable to understand and react. It also builds up tension that needs to be emptied equally by emotions—now with joy. It is the body's return to a healthy balance.

We have feelings and emotions because we understand some things, but we don't understand others. If we understood everything, we would also have no emotions. Emotions are closely linked to the unknown, the doubtful, the ambiguous, and the uncertain. There are no emotions regarding what we know or are totally unaware of. What is fully conscious or unconscious does not move.

Emotions can be pleasant or unpleasant, but they are all adaptive; that is, they guide us towards our survival. Emotions are like a complex communication system, which regulates how we interact with the environment.

The basic emotions are Joy, Love, Surprise, Wrath, Sadness, and Fear. Each of these emotions has a function. They are like "software" that serves not only to communicate, but to propel the action, and fast.

In most everyday situations, these behaviors are extremely useful to us. For example, if we see a snake, fear (it has the function of protection and survival) will tell us to flee; if we lose a loved one, sadness (it has the function of personal reintegration, "motivates us to") guides us to leave work and stay at home to seek "support"; when we are happy we are more willing to explore and try new situations, it is easier to plan and make decisions faster, etc.

But sometimes, our emotions get deregulated in patterns that don't help us. For example, fear pushes us to run away from everything, the sadness of withdrawing from activities that help us to feel better, and shame (feeling secondary to sadness) to hide from everything, so that we never have any chance of getting away from it.

The impulses to avoid emotional discomfort at all costs can make our lives difficult: when we avoid undesirable emotions, we end up losing all the dimensions that animate them too. This is when we need to activate our brain's highest level, the prefrontal cortex, to reflect: Do these emotions push us in a useful direction? Are they allowing us to live the full life that we want to live?

If the answer is no, our prefrontal cortex, the anatomical structure of the brain most recently developed in the evolutionary process, where functions such as complex thoughts, behavior planning, personality expression, decision making or modulation of social behavior reside, overlap up to our limbic system ("emotions," the amygdala, the "emotional heart" responsible for emotional processing, or the acquisition of fear responses, playing a central role in the body's alarm and reaction responses to certain stimuli). This pushes us to act in the opposite direction of how we feel, even if we are really uncomfortable at the moment.

Why Are Some People More Emotional Than Others?

People are unique and different from each other, there is no doubt, but some are much more intense and, when something negative happens, they despair, cry, suffer. When something good takes over, they skip around the world. On the other hand, there are those who react more sparingly. I wonder why?

A new study suggests that this difference in the emotional reaction may have to do with genetic issues. For this, tests were carried out to assess the processing of emotions within the brain, which may explain why some people are more susceptible to post-traumatic stress, for example.

People really see the world differently. For those who have this genetic variation, the emotionally relevant things in the world stand out much more.

Hereditary

The studied gene is ADRA2b, responsible for the regulation of the neurotransmitter norepinephrine. According to another research leader, Professor Adam Anderson, emotions are not processed purely in the way they happen but are also influenced by the way the brain perceives them.

Anderson explains that it shows us that our genes really interfere with how we view the positive and negative aspects of life and that some people tend to see bad experiences as major threats.

Todd explains that although it seems bad to have more intense responses to emotions, the truth is that this can have its positive side too, as this genetic variation helps people who react with more emotion to realize what is, in fact, relevant in the world. She cites Marcel Proust as an example of a highly sensitive person who transformed what he felt into creativity and literary production of excellent quality. Now tell us: what type of person do you fit in with?

Useful Tips

When building relationships with others, you should pay particular attention to what type of people they are. What for? It's simple: to interact with emotional people, you need one approach, and with logical people—another.

For example, a logical person in decision-making is more guided by facts, figures, depth of evidence, and other reasonable parameters that lead him to the goal. And an emotional person, on the contrary, pays more attention to the states that he lives in the moment and which, having reached the goal, he will experience. A large amount of data and numbers can confuse or alienate.

Objectively, it is important to understand that both logical and emotional people experience emotions. Believe me; piss off, piss yourself off, touch, inspire, make laugh and various other feelings can be evoked with anyone. It's just that logical people have lesser feelings and emotions, and pushing them to the impulses of the soul will be noticeably more difficult than those who, from birth, are more likely to reveal their inner world to others.

And one more important point. Emotional people, in contrast to logical ones, make most decisions at the level of emotions. They are more susceptible to psychological effects. This is a payment for their creativity and profundity of life perception, because they see the world from a different angle, not like logical people.

The Roots of Empathy

Empathy is built on self-awareness. The more we open ourselves to our own thoughts, the more capable we will be of reading other people's feelings.

The alexithymic, who do not know their feelings, feel lost when it comes to knowing what someone who is with them feels.

They are emotionally deaf. The notes and chords of emotion, which slip into people's words and actions, the revealing tone of voice or change of posture, the eloquent silence or a revealing tremor, go unnoticed.

Confused about their feelings, alexithymic are equally bewildered when other people express theirs to them.

This inability to register the feelings of another is a significant deficit of emotional intelligence and a tragic failure in what it means to be human. Because all rapport, the root of interest in someone arises from emotional attunement, from the capacity for empathy.

That ability, the ability to know what someone else is feeling, comes into play in a wide range of life situations. From sales and administration to idyll and parenthood, through compassion and political activity.

The absence of empathy is also revealing; it exists in psychopaths, criminals, abductors, and child molesters.

People's emotions are seldom expressed in words; much more often, they are manifested through other signals. The key to intuiting another's feelings is in the ability to interpret non-verbal channels: tone of voice, gestures, facial expression, and the like.

Just as the rational mind expresses itself through words, the expression of emotions is nonverbal. When a person's words conflict with what is manifested through tone of voice, gestures, or other non-verbal channels, emotional truth lies in the way the person communicates something, rather than what they say.

A rule of thumb used in communications research holds that 90 percent or more of an emotional message is nonverbal.

Those messages, the anxiety in the tone of voice, the irritation in the abruptness of a gesture, are almost always perceived unconsciously, without paying specific attention to the nature of the message, but receiving and responding tacitly.

The skills that allow us to do this right or wrong are also, for the most part, tacitly learned.

In general, women are better than men for this kind of empathy (Daniel Goleman).

Managing with Heart

We are talking about those who are cold, have very little compassion, and may even appear indolent. These are people who have a heart so hard that few emotions seem to be able to cross their borders and cross the layer of consciousness. We are, of course, referring to ice hearts.

Eyes that won't cry, lips that don't usually smile, hands that don't touch. To those who never give up their role as spectators, who give the impression that nothing that happens to them is important to them. However, these people are fragile while they do everything to appear strong.

We sometimes hide behind a shell, thinking that we will no longer feel the pain, but we do not see that by isolating ourselves, we are already hurting ourselves.

How are ice hearts?

When we talk about "ice hearts," we are looking at those who find it difficult to express how they feel. Here are some of their features:

- **Assumption.** These people may think that others already know how they are feeling. Therefore, they stop showing it.
- **Perfectionists.** They find it difficult to admit that they make mistakes. Besides, being weak is one of them.
- **Low self-esteem.** This prevents them from showing their feelings; they think that they have little or no value and therefore believe that it is useless to express themselves.
- **Fear.** They can be people who are afraid of facing conflicts and showing their emotions.
- **Catastrophic thinking.** They may also end up believing that everything is lost in advance. So what is the point of fighting?
- **Ignoring.** These people may not know how to communicate properly.

- **Timidity.** People with a heart of ice can hide how they feel to protect themselves. They use it as a defense mechanism against the possibility of being vulnerable.
- **Difficulty feeling.** They find it difficult to listen to themselves and, therefore, to determine what they feel.

Ice hearts have many feelings

Each person is a world. Those with ice hearts can display either of these characteristics. However, the common denominator of all these points is that they are unable to open a space for their emotions.

However, the fact that they do not express them does not mean that they do not feel them. People with a heart of ice have feelings, but the problem is that they don't know or don't want to communicate them. The mechanisms that drive them to do so may be conscious or unconscious.

But how do ice hearts work? These people can be strong or distant. They, therefore, give the impression of being insensitive.

There can indeed be people as cold as ice cubes, so much so that they do not feel the slightest compassion or empathy for others. These people suffer from psychopathy. However, not all ice hearts are like this. As we have already explained, some are so out of timidity, fear, perfection, etc.

How to manage your emotions?

It is important to learn to manage your emotions. Why? Because we then become more assertive in our relationships, with ourselves and with others. Let's see how to get there:

Accept our feelings. Recognizing and accepting our emotions will help us grow and get to know each other better.

We focus on self-esteem. When we recognize our worth, we realize our importance. This will help us to know that our emotions are just as important. We can, therefore, focus on them when necessary, to grow as people, and improve our relationships.

Release. Sometimes when shyness rules us, we lock ourselves in prison and throw the key out because of this anxiety, which arises from the meeting with the other.

Face our fears. We may be afraid; however, in addition to recognizing this fear, we need to understand why it arises and why we let it out. By doing this, it will be easier for us to express what we feel. On the other hand, if we leave opinions aside and stop assuming that others will react in this or that way, we will more easily experience authentic moments and will be able to express ourselves without pressure.

Try to express our emotions. When we have spent a good part of our lives, not showing what we are feeling, starting to express our emotions can seem extremely difficult. So, to make this task a little easier, we can start by doing it with understanding people who are close to us.

Self-awareness. By getting to know each other, we will be able to identify our emotions and express them assertively more easily.

Emotions form a real universe. Managing them is not an easy task, but neither is it an impossible challenge. The main thing is to recognize them, to live them, to know how to express them, and when.

We are not all the same. Everyone expresses their emotions in a particular way. However, there is one thing to watch out for: this accumulation of feelings can end up suffocating us.

Putting ice hearts aside: the benefits

When we talk about "putting ice hearts aside," we

are not talking about people but the stiff, cold hearts that we sometimes have. This will bring us great benefits. Here are a few:

- Reduced anxiety
- Increased empathy
- Reduced stress
- Better self-awareness
- Strengthening relationships with others and with ourselves
- Improved self-esteem
- Better assertive communication

To be able to know these benefits, it is good to follow or to have followed certain educational practices from an early age. These help us to become more aware of our emotions. This is what Arís Redo suggests in his article for the journal Vivat Academia, in which he explains the importance of emotional education for teachers and students.

If it is true that there are people with hearts of ice, that does not mean that it is impossible to soften them. Through emotional management, they will become more assertive when expressing their emotions, and, little by little, they will remove this heavy armor that makes them seem insensitive.

How to Get the Best out of People

Surely at some point in your life, you have been frustrated because you saw how someone with great human potential was not giving you his best. Even some disappointment may have led you to wonder if it is enough to put the best in one to be able to bring out the best in the other.

The truth is that when we talk about interpersonal relationships, although we cannot always put a label on that relationship, everything positive adds up. In some cases, perhaps we will not be able to promote the relationship so that it is as good as we would like since the last word is from the other, but we will get closer.

Remember that the important thing is that the other treats us to the best of his ability, although sometimes he is not able to contribute as much as we would like. Patience, in this case, can be an ally, let's remember that relationships also need to develop and grow to shine.

You deserve as much as the others

In our relations with others, it is convenient not to demand the exact fulfillment of our wishes, since this demand may have the opposite effect. Think that a healthy relationship is one in which both parties feel completely conditioned and even lacking in freedom. Instead, putting your best foot forward with flexibility and patience may be the best invitation for others to do the same for you.

And isn't it true that, whether in a friendship, in a loving relationship, or even a family one, we feel loved when we both strive? Taking this reciprocity into account is also beneficial to us: just as you put your best foot forward, you are also able to see equitable behavior in the other.

The balance of the asymmetrical relationship will help us to develop the best version of ourselves in it, even unconsciously. This will mean that we perceive that the other person is worthwhile and that we form a good team.

Putting the best of yourself is a sign of trust

Stephen Covey said that "if you want to awaken trust, you must be trustworthy," and indeed, for others to open up, we may have to be the first to embrace one-way. Do not be afraid to do it, since knowing your fears and your virtues will make others place their trust in you to reveal theirs, and it is very gratifying that someone considers us worthy of it.

Being able to do your best means being confident enough to know that those inner fears, shortcomings, or darkness are not big enough to overshadow all the good we can offer. So do not fear, since knowing and valuing yourself will allow those around you to see every one of your virtues.

"Trust is a two-way road," he said harshly.

"What are you suggesting?"

"That trust cannot be demanded when it is not granted."

- Dolores Redondo, from Legacy in the Bones-

Everyone will appreciate your trust in you, and therefore they will feel safe in your company: in the ties we have, a kind of closed circle is created in which several people move in unison and the edges soften.

Offer without interest, receive with gratitude

We all know the saying, "each one collects what he sows. " Have you ever felt that way? We may not see results in the short term in putting the best of ourselves, but in the long run, it will be another reason for happiness.

First, how good it feels to give; secondly, because our relationships will be stronger; thirdly, because others will give themselves to us honestly and without asking.

Probably, once we have experienced this feeling with the rest and they have also done it with us: if we continually demand and do not recognize what they do to make us feel better, they will end up having a hard time giving us everything they could. However, usually, others do their best when they see that we do it too.

Discovering what is inside those we love is as nice as realizing what is in ours. Reciprocity is the key between two people who strive to maintain strong and healthy ties: it ends up becoming what saves us—as Neruda would say—from life, love.

CHAPTER 11

THE ART OF PERSUASION

Persuasion is not just about discovering a person's emotional profile. You have to look for unsatisfied emotions and give them a way out. Listen to what they are concerned about and come up with solutions. Persuasion, in a sense, is also a task that involves creating a desire in others.

Whether it is about closing a deal, asking for a fee increase, motivating a sales team of 5,000 people, negotiating on an individual basis, acquiring a new company, or scrapping an outdated one, situations, contingencies or conjunctures almost always come down to relationship problems and personal treatment.

These unavoidable problems of relationship and personal treatment require persuasive action for their correct resolution since the other paths involve the curtailment of the freedom of others, such as threats, coercion, the use of force, etc.

Persuasion is necessary because individuals, communities, nations, often have different interests, customs, points of view, etc. When the achievement of one person's goals is blocked by the behavior of another in pursuit of their goal, persuasion is used to convince the offender to redefine his goal or modify the means to achieve it.

Persuasion is necessary because there is resistance. To resist is to oppose a force or a body to the action or violence of another force or another body. Many physical phenomena are based on resistance, and thanks to them, we can live. Why do you resist? On the mental plane, resistance is also an inevitable phenomenon: through resistance, we create lasting impressions, impact, persuade, convince, and negotiate.

Resistance, on the psychological plane, is illustrated by the principle of "cognitive dissonance." Psychologists call "cognitive dissonance" the phenomenon by which our minds instinctively reject the possibility of containing two opposing thoughts or beliefs.

Therefore, in our human relationships, we exchange dissimilar thoughts, feelings, and beliefs that resist each other. That is why all human beings exercise resistance. And when you study why you resist yourself, you understand why others resist.

And that understanding is very important because it doesn't seem very skillful to resist resistance. As the repetition of the words themselves seems to graph it, it is like "condemning a sentence," or "shouting saying that one should not shout." Resistance must be allowed to flow, that is, it must be allowed its full expression, even allowing it to reach its limit.

The resistance is moderated with "lubricants," with "shock absorbers," listening and giving space to the other. Resistance is a thought, almost always accompanied by a feeling. By subtly changing that thought, resistance can disappear.

The First Element of Persuasion is nothing but influence. And the influence begins with what matters to your potential ally. Professor Harry Overstreet, in his illustrative book Influencing Human Behavior, says: ´Action stems from what we fundamentally want (…) and the best advice that can be given to those who seek to be persuasive, whether in business, at home, at school or in politics, it is this: first, to awaken in the neighbor a frank desire. Whoever can do this has the whole world with him— those who cannot walk alone along the way. Therefore, the strength of mutual exchange consists in obtaining what one wants and giving others what they need.'

Persuasion is a mere intellectual exercise: How to persuade is to make the feelings and ideas that we would like them to have appeared in the spirit of another or other people. And we must always keep in mind that our actions do not come only from abstract reasons, cultural patterns, etc. They mainly come from our desires, interests, and emotions.

If I could describe in one sentence the art of persuasion, that phrase would be the following: persuasion is to convert people, not in our way of thinking, but in our way of feeling and believing.

People do things for emotional reasons. Therefore, persuading is also influencing the emotional attitudes of others.

Persuasion is not just about discovering a person's emotional profile. You have to look for unsatisfied emotions and give them a way out. Listen to what they are concerned about and come up with solutions. Persuasion, in a sense, is also a task that involves creating a desire in others.

The History of Persuasion

Do you know what a speech by Barack Obama, an announcement by Chanel, a gamification campaign for the VW Polo, and a press release by Repsol have in common? The answer is found in work written over 2,300 years ago! Its title is The Rhetoric and the author, Aristotle. This treaty establishes the foundations of corporate advertising, political, institutional, emotional, and journalistic communication.

Through this Section, we will try to discover how the theoretical precepts and the methodology exposed in The Rhetoric are applied daily and in a multidisciplinary way in the areas of professional communication. The conceptual basis of the work revolves around the command of the word and discourse—discursiveness—as instruments to exercise persuasive communication. Along with these elements are the arguments or reasoning that will be presented to the public to convince them by appealing to their feelings and emotions. Likewise, Aristotle determines and analyzes the protagonists of this process: sender, receiver, message, and channel or medium.

The issue is you must project an image of credibility, authority, and moderation that facilitates the acceptance of your messages by the interlocutor. As for the recipient, it will be essential to know their approximate age and social status. In this way, the contents will be adapted to the particularities of the audience. El message is characterized by a simple style but elaborate. However not conveying the feeling of artificiality. The vocabulary will be clear and intelligible for all audiences.

And the use of 'linguistic' resources that attract the attention of the interlocutor will be pertinent. Aristotle defines the structure of the messages in preamble, proposition, and epilogue. The preamble will capture the attention of the public to present the topic that will be addressed later. In the proposition, all the argumentative and narrative force of the exhibition will be overturned. The epilogue will contain a synopsis to summarize and consolidate the transmitted message. The message will appeal to the rational and emotional component that predisposes the interlocutor in a sense desired by the sender. Finally, it specifies that the message and its structures will always be adapted to the channel or medium through which it is transmitted.

As a result, this section constitutes a look at the past that takes us back to the original concepts of persuasion. This appeal is relevant in the prevailing digital environment in which we are located. In fact, at present, we use the infinity of supports and technological channels that are within our reach. Thus, we are present in traditional social networks

(Facebook, Twitter, Instagram, Pinterest, YouTube, etc.) and other emerging ones (Periscope, Meerkat). And we are up to date with private messaging systems like Telegram and innovative applications like Snapchat. Of course, we know the trends in the creation of branded content (storytelling, scroll telling, etc.)

And we try to approach the public through personalized, gamified, and quality themes, thus developing the cross-cutting nature of the information. But, simultaneously, we must not forget that the means—technological support—is not the end, but must be a tool in the exercise of our profession. And we must remember that assertion of the classical thinkers: 'the oldest is the most modern.' Past and present shake hands, since the final objective—to guide, influence the interlocutor's will using persuasive stimuli and appealing to his emotions—continues to be the same twenty-three centuries later.

Psychological Trick to Get People to Say Yes

Each of us, at least once in our life, thought about what would happen if we could become the ruler of the whole world. Often we want our opinion for other people to be perceived as the only correct one. We want people close to us always to be able to help in any situation. To realize all this, we all ask the same question - How to make a person say "yes" to us? In this chapter, you will see a couple of tricks, thanks to which people will not be able to pass by you and your requests.

Here we go!

"The one for whom you have done good is ready to answer you with even greater good," said the famous American politician Benjamin Franklin. A series of different experiments show that if we render a service to a person, he can almost immediately tell us "yes" to our request, or he can take the initiative in his own hands and offer to do something for you. This is because the person for whom we rendered the service does not want to remain "in debt," even if we deliberately warned him that we did not need anything. It will be much easier for him to agree to your request, no matter how financially or psychologically expensive it is.

When you are talking with someone and want to receive a positive response to your request, mention the name of that person as often as possible. There is no greater delight for a person's ears than repeating his name in a conversation. In this way a person understands how important he can be for you and how much the fulfillment of your request depends on his answer.

Always overstate your requirements and requests. Yes, it is very likely that if I now ask my friend for 10 thousand as a loan, she will refuse me. But after a while, the friend's guilt will take up, because she will begin to realize that I needed the money for definitely urgent purposes, and with a 95% probability she will lend me a smaller amount, but it will turn out to be the same right amount. Overestimating our requests, we receive an immediate refusal, but then the person who refuses us offers us another condition, which is most optimal for use in the current situation.

It's much easier for us to say "yes" to someone we have sympathy for. Almost everyone is familiar with this trick, and just the same people use it most often. The phrases "You are my friend" or "We are friends with you, right?" increase the chance to get a positive answer at times because we appeal to the most expensive features that a person has—his conscience and relationships with others.

One of the features of a person is to relate well to those who are somehow similar to him. If we know the manner of communication and the character traits of our interlocutor, then we can begin to carefully "copy" them, but so that it doesn't catch the eye. Our interlocutor will begin to notice that you are similar in some ways, and with a further request, he will be happy to help.

Positively use gestures, i.e., constantly try to show how interesting the conversation is to you: nod, show something with gestures. A person will begin to notice that you are interested in a conversation that you are listening to him, which means that he will listen to your request.

Listening is one of the most important persuasion techniques. If a person only pretends that he is interested in conversation and only occasionally gives "signs of life," then this can be noticed right away, and you can't count on a positive answer.

Listen to what your interlocutor is talking about, and you are more likely to get a solid "yes" to your request.

How to build lasting Relationships

The quality of any relationship is hard to predict: often completely impossible relationships last for years, while others that seem to have all the advantages collapse. Nevertheless, the practice of marriage counseling and the analysis of the causes for marriage breakdown suggest that some factors predispose either to improve or break up relationships. If you are interested in your own chances of forming a successful partnership, consider some of the main factors below.

Do not bind yourself when you are too young. Early marriages are at greatest risk. Each serious study of marriage issues shows that marriages concluded before the age of 19 are least preserved (especially if the marriage is completed because the woman is already pregnant). As you reach maturity, you change, different needs and interests develop, diverging from partners. Two people can develop more or less in one direction, continuing to coordinate changing needs with each other, but much more often, they grow apart.

Do not commit too quickly. You should not decide to create long-term relationships until you know each other for at least nine months. It is this period that allows most people to find out each other's best aspects and shortcomings and, living together, in practice to find out whether the partnership will stand the test of time.

Violent involvement in sexual union is a sign of danger. If you often quarrel and especially if one of you repeatedly breaks your connection, this is a bad harbinger for the future, since such a behavior pattern tends to take root. Putting off formalizing relationships can also be worrying. If you agreed on a joint life, but postponed the design of permanent relations for a couple of years or more, carefully consider your motives. This may mean that you are not yet ready to give up your independence.

Look for similarities. Surveys show that there is a tendency to marry your own kind. Although some marriages of dissimilar people turn out to be successful, life together, not accompanied by friction, is easier for a couple who have common interests and views, who want to get the same thing from life. It is useful to have at least one or two "cross-cutting" interests, as well as match each other in age. If the difference between you is more than ten years, it is likely that such differences of opinion will be inevitable that will create excessive difficulties for the normal development of relations.

Look for harmony between the sexes. Gender does not display its intrinsic binding power if your opinions on it are somewhat different or if in your life it plays a far greater (or much smaller) role than in your partner's life. Sexual compatibility is not a technological problem, because in the course of mutual adaptation the "mechanics" of love can be discovered. It is much more important that there is a real attraction to each other and a mutually stimulating effect, only on this basis can each of you fully satisfy the sexual needs of the other. On the basis of mutual attraction and love, almost all sexual problems are solvable, and without it, they are likely to be insurmountable.

Searches for emotional maturity. Some personality traits are extremely harmful to long-term relationships in the future. Anger is probably the most potentially destructive force for a lasting relationship in the future. Perhaps a violent clash with a partner who is trying to dominate is an aggressive and malicious tendency. If you can still hope that the relationship will remain with one psychologically immature partner, then with two, they are irrevocably doomed to failure. Low self-esteem also does not bode well, as it creates insecurity and jealousy, making it difficult to create relationships based on love and trust.

A mature and long-term relationship may not be possible if you are overly addicted. A partner who remains highly dependent on parents may require more support from you than you are willing or able to provide. In certain circumstances, when you need assistance, even temporary, he may not be able to take the burden of responsibility on his shoulders as a mature person.

Make sure your partner can provide you with physical intimacy and emotional support. A person who is emotionally isolated and who is difficult to show feelings or accept them physically has few prospects for maintaining a full relationship.

The search for flexibility. The ability to adapt to change is one of the most important features that must be considered when choosing a partner. Neither individuals nor couples remain unchanged, and an uncompromising person may have difficulty meeting with changing needs and circumstances of a long-term relationship. It's good if your current or potential partner agrees to think over new ideas or try new forms of activity.

If you have serious doubts about this relationship, do not have the hope that your partner will change. Hoping that under your influence, he will become less gloomy or extravagant, less angry, and not so prone to jealousy, you doom yourself to a significant risk. Some people have great potential for change, others the other way around. Thus, if the ability to change is essential for you, and you look for your partner's signs and do it before, rather than after, you have seriously linked yourself to a close relationship.

111

It is your own confidence in the existing relationship and the resulting determination to translate your intentions into reality. If you have doubts, they will intensify, preventing you from completely surrendering to creating relationships that could help overcome all problems and survive.

CHAPTER 12

SOCIAL INFLUENCE

Social influence occurs when a person has emotions, opinions, or behaviors that affect others intentionally or unintentionally. There are multiple types of social influence and can be considered as consistent, socialization, peer pressure, obedience, leadership, persuasion, sales, and marketing. In 1958, Harvard psychologist Herbert Kelman identified three-wide varieties of social influence.

- Conformity, when it comes to people, agree with another matter itself to keep their particular opinions private.
- Identification is when people are influenced by someone who is loved and respected, such as a celebrity.
- Internationalization is when people accept faith or behavior and agree as publicly as privately.

Morton Deutsch and Harold Gerard have identified two psychological needs that lead people to live up to others' expectations. They include our need to be right (informational social influence) and our need to be loved (normative social influence). Information

Impact (or Social Evidence) is the influence of accepting information from another as evidence of reality. Informational impact comes into play when people are not sure, either because the incentives are internally ambiguous or because there are social differences. Regulatory impact: so that they meet the positive expectations of others. From Kelman's typology, regulatory influence leads to public compliance, while information impact leads to private acceptance.

Types

Social influence is a broad term that refers to many different phenomena. Listed below are some of the main types of social influence that are currently being researched in the field of social psychology.

Kelman varieties

There are three processes of attitudinal change, as defined by Harvard psychologist Herbert Kelman in a 1958 article published in the journal Conflict Resolution. The purpose of defining these processes is to help determine the influence of social influence: for example, to separate social correspondence (behavior) from private reception (personal faith).

Compliance

Compliance is the act of satisfying an explicit or implicit request proposed by others. From a technical point of view, compliance is a change in behavior, but not necessarily in relation; it can be performed because of simple obedience or otherwise prefers to retain personal thoughts due to social pressure. According to article 1958 of Kelman, the satisfaction received from compliance is determined by the social effect of the host influence (i.e., people are responsible for the expected reward or punishment, disgust).

Identification

Identification is a change in attitude or behavior due to the influence of someone who is admired. Ads that rely on celebrity endorsements to market their products take advantage of this phenomenon. According to Kelman, the required relationship is that the identifier refers to a behavior or attitude change.

Internationalization

Internationalization is the process of adopting many norms established by people or groups that affect the individual. A person accepts influence because the content of the influence accepted is internally useful.

This is comparable to an individual's value system, and according to Kelman, the "reward" of internalization is the "content of new behavior."

Conformity

Conformity is a type of social influence associated with changing behavior, beliefs, or thinking to align with other states or with regulatory standards. This is the most common form of social influence. Social psychology research in accordance, as a rule, distinguish between two varieties: information correspondence (also called social evidence, or "internalization" in Kelman terms), and normative correspondence ("correspondence" from Kelman's point of view).

In the case of peer pressure, the person is convinced to do what they may not want to do (for example, take drugs), but which they perceive as "necessary" to maintain a positive attitude with other people (for example, their friends). Correspondence from peer pressure is usually the result of identification with group members or with the observance of some members to reassure others.

Compliance may be in appearance or may be more complete, influencing an individual both publicly and privately.

Correspondence (also referred to as mute) demonstrates the public conformity of the group to the majority or norms. At the same time, the individual continues to disagree privately or dissent, holding on to his initial beliefs or an alternative set of beliefs that are different from the majority. Correspondence appears as conformity, but there is a separation between the public and private self.

The conversion involves the private recognition of what is missing in compliance. Coordinating the original behavior, belief, or change in the thinking of the individual with that of others (influencing), both publicly and privately. A person has adopted behavior, beliefs, or thinking, and assimilates it by doing it on his own. The transformation may also apply to individual group members, changing from their initial (and diverse) opinions to accepting the opinions of others, which may differ from their original opinions. As a consequence, the group's stance can be a combination of various aspects of initial individual views, or it can be an alternative based on the initial positions reached by consensus.

What seems to match in reality may be coherence. Coherence occurs when an individual's behavior, faith, or thought is already aligned with the activities of others, and no changes occur.

In situations where there is no conformity (including conformity, transformation, and comparison), there are non-conformity processes, such as independence and anti-conformity. Independence, also referred to as dissent, includes an individual (either through his actions or inaction, or through a public expression of his beliefs or thinking) aligned with their standards, but incompatible with other members of the group (or all groups or the majority). Anti-conformity, also referred to as the counter-argument of conformity, may appear as independence, but it lacks consistency with personal standards and to challenge the group. Actions, as well as reported views and beliefs, are often contradictory to group norm or majority norm.

Minority influence

The influence of a minority occurs when the majority is influenced by the belief or behavior of the minority. The influence of a minority may depend on the size of the majority and minority, the level of coherence of the minority group, and situational factors (such as the affluence or social significance of the minority). The influence of a minority most often acts through informational social influence (as opposed to normative social influence), since the majority can be indifferent to the soul of the minority.

Prophecy itself

Prophecy is a prediction that directly or indirectly calls itself to become true because of the positive feedback between faith and behavior. The prophecy is proclaimed as truth (when it is a lie), may influence a person enough, either by fear or logical misunderstanding, so that their reaction eventually fulfills a false prophecy once. This term is attributed to the sociologist Robert C. Merton from an article he published in 1948.

Reactance

Reactive is the acceptance of a vision contrary to the belief that a person is under pressure to accept, perhaps because of an alleged threat to behavioral freedom. This phenomenon is also called anticonformity. Although the results are the opposite of what the Influencer intends, reactive behavior is the result of social pressure. It should be noted that anticonformity does not necessarily mean independence. In many studies, reactance manifests itself in the deliberate rejection of influence, even if the influence is correct.

Humility

Obedience is a form of social influence, derived from

an authoritative figure. The Milgram experiment, the Zimbardo Stanford prison experiment, and the Höfling hospital experiment are three particularly well-known obedience experiments. And they all conclude that people are surprisingly obedient in the presence of perceived figures of legitimate authorities.

Persuasiveness

Persuasion is the process of directing oneself or others towards accepting relationships by rational or symbolic means. Cialdini identified six "weapons of influence": reciprocity, commitment, social proof, authority, taste, and rarity. This is a "weapon of influence" of an attempt to achieve correspondence of directed means. Persuasion can occur through calls for rationality or calls for emotion.

Psychological manipulation

Psychological manipulation is a form of social control that attempts to alter other people's behavior or attitude through strategies that are offensive, deceptive, or behind-the-scenes. These strategies may be called exploitative, coercive, manipulative, and misleading by promoting the manipulator's interests, often at the detriment of another.

Social influence does not inherently have a negative effect. For example, doctors may try to convince patients to change bad habits. Social influence is generally perceived as harmless when it respects the right to accept or reject it adversely and is not too coercive. Depending on the context and motivation, social influence may constitute backroom manipulations.

Offensive Nutrition and Management

Controlling rapists use tactics to exercise power and control over their victims. The abuser aims to manipulate and threaten the victim, or to force them to believe they have no fair voice in the relationship.

Propaganda

Advocacy is information that is not objective and is primarily used to influence the audience and further the list, often presenting facts selectively encouraging a particular synthesis or perception. Or use a loaded language to produce an emotional response to the information presented, rather than a rational one.

Hard power

Strong power is the use of military and economical means to control certain political bodies' actions or desires. This form of political power is always violent (coercion), and is most successful when it is enforced on another lesser military and economic force by one political entity. Hard power is in contrast to a soft power derived from politics, culture, and tradition.

Emotions

Emotions and disposition can affect an individual's likelihood of matching or anticonformity. In 2009, a study found that fear increases the likelihood of agreement with the group, while romance or lust increases the chances of going against the group.

Social networks

A social network is a social system composed of nodes (representing individuals or organizations) linked (through ties, also called edges, ties, or links) by one or more forms of interdependencies (e.g., friendship, shared interests, or values, sexual relationships, or kinship). The study of the social network uses the network theory lens to research social relations. An analysis of social networks as a field has become more visible since the mid-20th century in determining the channels and consequences of social influence. For example, Christakis and Fowler found that social networks convey status and behavior, such as obesity, smoking, drinking, and happiness.

Determining the degree of social influence, based on large-scale observational data from a latent social network structure, is related to various collective social phenomena, including crimes, civil unrest, and voter behavior in elections. For example, methodologies for unraveling the social influence of peers from external influences—with a latent social network structure and large-scale—were data applied by US observant presidential elections, stock markets, and civil unrest.

CHAPTER 13

THE ART OF BODY LANGUAGE

Body language is a non-verbal communication channel that allows you to see what the other person is thinking about. A lot of manuals have been written on body language because this topic is quite extensive and fascinating; Those who wish can study them on their own. In this chapter, the applied use of body language is considered only in one area of interest to us.

A person in defense often stands in a closed position, with a cross of arms, and even legs.

Deviation of the body back and a large distance in communication more often indicates that the person does not trust you, does not consider you completely his own.

Touching a person's nose often indicates that a person doubts something, and a woman's correction of her curls in front of a man usually indicates that she rather likes the man.

Why learn body language?

People who set the task with the help of sign

124

language to calculate those who will deceive and manipulate them do not protect themselves with this knowledge. The programs that teach "to recognize fraudsters and manipulators" lead to the exact opposite result: the number of people deceived as a result of these programs is only growing. Nevertheless, to understand sign language (more broadly—body language) is necessary; this is a natural moment of the general psychological culture. Knowledge of gestures is not a block or a master key, but a bridge to people and proximity.

Body language and the relationship between soul and body

Body language is not interested in body features that speak about the individual characteristics of a person, about his potential, about the possibilities of his growth and development. Body language does not always indicate what is happening in the soul, and often it's just a cultural or social convention. The science of body language is the science of non-verbal communication. About how, observing a person's body and gestures, to unravel what a person is hiding from us. Or how to use a body, without actually speaking, using the capabilities of gestures, facial expressions, and intonations, to convey to him some message from us.

Interpretation of gestures and gait

Human gestures are very diverse. To learn how to interpret them, it is necessary to understand for what purposes this or that movement serves. Gestures in the process of communication perform four main functions. First, they replace words with signs. You will probably understand the person you are talking to if he wants to say "OK" without words, showing you the thumb and forefinger connected. Secondly, they control the attention of the interlocutor and clarify what was said. If you need to show where the store that a passerby asks you about is, instead of long explanations, you will show with your hand the direction where he needs to go. Thirdly, they illustrate and reinforce what has been said. When the fisherman shows what kind of fish he caught, he will show it to you with his hands, and whether you believe the scope of his hands is up to you. Well, and fourthly, gestures adapt a person's body to the process of communication or express a person's state. Crossed arms create a state of security for a person, and lowered shoulders indicate that a person is tired or has lost faith in himself... It is these gestures that are most interesting for interpretation, and it is most difficult to interpret them since many of them are individual and often unrecognized. Nevertheless, it is quite possible to give some clues.

Interpretation of facial expressions

Simple emotions, expressive movements (joy, surprise, resentment) are easily understood, but in other cases, interpreting and decoding facial expressions can be a daunting task requiring attention, knowledge, and professionalism. When interpreting facial movements, it is important to adhere to the following rules:

1) Observe facial expressions in dynamics. "Video is always more informative than the photo."

2) For interpretation, it is necessary to track at least three parameters of facial expressions.

3) A statement about the emotions experienced by a person should be formulated in a hypothetical form. For example, "Based on the observed mimic movements (the eyes are wide, the muscles of the forehead are stretched in an upward movement, the lips are half-open, the corners of the lips are raised), we observe the face of a person who is more enthusiastic than calm."

Sleep and body language

The falling asleep and sleeping person chooses this or that position of a body depending on the personal features and a state at the given moment.

The Five C's of Body Language

Body language Communication strategies are essential for companies to obtain good results. It is necessary to know the client and that the client knows the company and its products, and it is the responsibility of the company to know how to communicate it well. Several points can help with this task. They are known as the 5 C's of effective Body language communication.

- **Control:** there needs to be self-control in the communicator, both in body language and in verbal language.
- **Conversation:** more than a speech, the listener must have the feeling that he is having a conversation that is bringing him new and interesting knowledge. Otherwise, you can get bored and not get the message across.
- **Confidence:** it is an important C in many situations, but when it comes to communicating a message, it is even more so. If you want the speaker to believe what you are saying, you must also believe it yourself.
- **Competence:** you have to show a professional attitude that conveys that you have full knowledge of the topic or product you are talking about. To transmit a message

effectively, there has to be a product behind it.

- **Calm:** anyone who speaks calmly tends to transmit that same calm to the rest and therefore creates an environment of greater receptivity to what is being said.

Extra

Clarity: being clear is essential. The more an argument is bundled, the worse the message will get to the interlocutors. It is best not to overdo the subject and go directly to the fundamental idea.

The interlocutor will appreciate having time to discuss or ask questions on the subject, for that you have to express the message concisely and leave time for the rest.

Mastering the Secrets of Non-Verbal Communication

If you want more performance in your presentations, relying on non-verbal communication will increase your chances of success. Check out the secrets to being successful with this technique.

Communicating clearly and effectively is essential during presentations, either to your classmates or to a team of executives at work. However, relying only on words is not the most recommended method of seeking success in your way of communicating. You've got to rely on another tool to be successful: non-verbal communication. Although it is despised by many, non-verbal communication techniques can contribute greatly to the efficiency of presentation.

Eye Contact

To ensure efficient non-verbal communication, you must make eye contact. If you are in a presentation, you can use much more than words to express the importance of what you are saying. Try to make eye contact with as many presents as possible in your presentation, and this will make them take what you are saying seriously.

Voice fluctuation

Another way to emphasize what you are saying is to use your voice as a resource. A monotonous and constant tone will make people distracted, regardless of the content of your presentation. If you know the right time to increase or decrease your tone of voice, emphasize one word or another and even pause, your viewer's attention will be completely focused on you.

Positioning

Like the monotonous tone of voice, standing next to

your presentation will make it boring. If you want to make your viewers interested in what you have to say, be dynamic. Walk around and in front of the room, point out examples. And never, under any circumstances, make your presentation sitting behind the computer. This is a bad practice.

Facial Expressions

For your audience to be enthusiastic about what you do, it is essential that you get excited about presenting it. If you stay with the famous "wake man" for as long as you are in front of them, there is no reason for them to feel the least bit interested in the subject. If you show how exciting the topic can be, more and more people will pay attention to the topic discussed. So, smile at the right moments, show animation, and even features of annoyance if that is the case.

Gestures

It is useless to walk around the room while presenting if your hands are kept in your pockets, crossed, or stuck to your sides. This shows discomfort. It makes people feel insecure about you. Try to count on the help of gestures; remember that your hands are not still during normal conversation. Just be careful not to overuse the feature and become a reason for jokes.

How to Interpret Verbal Communication

If we are more aware of this communication and understand what it means, we can better understand the people with whom we interact. This fact allows us to communicate more efficiently, and we can improve our communication with others and be more aware of what they are transmitting to us.

Sometimes we send out contradictory messages: we say one thing, but our body reveals a different message. This non-verbal language can affect how we act and how others react to us.

Situations where signs and signals will allow us to communicate more effectively:

First impression: trust

Remember, for example, the day you met a new coworker. What was your first impression? Did it give you confidence? Would you associate with him/her? Did he convince you? Did he walk steadily into the office, keep his gaze on you, shake your hand firmly, or did he come in with hardly a sound, look away, and extend a weak hand? While you were talking, was he keeping your gaze, or was he looking away? Did his face look relaxed or tense? What were the movements of his arms, broad gestures, or rather close to the body?

When you look at other people, it is easy to identify cues that show how that person is feeling at the moment, either through posture or tone of voice. If you are about to enter a situation where you do not feel as safe as you would like, for example, to give a conference or attend an important meeting, try to adopt these signs and signals that project confidence:

- Posture - forehead high, shoulders back.
- Eye contact - solid with a "smiling" face.
- Hand and arm gestures - determined.
- Speech - slow and clear.
- The tone of voice - moderate to low.

A difficult meeting: tension

Think of a time when you've been in a tough meeting—perhaps an evaluation, a negotiation of deadlines, responsibilities, or a contract.

In an ideal world, both you and the other person should be open and receptive to listening to what the other has to say to end the meeting successfully. However, the other person may be on the defensive and is not listening.

For this reason, it is important to identify if your interlocutor is receptive to what you are saying. How do you know if your message is falling on "deaf ears"? Some of the signs that identify the person they are talking to are on the defensive include:

- The gestures of the hand and arm are small and are kept close to the body.
- The facial expressions are minimal.
- The person is physically away from you.
- Crossed arms in front of their body.
- Their eyes maintain little contact or avoid your gaze.

In interpreting these signals, it is wise to change what is being said and how it is being said to help the other person feel more comfortable and more receptive to what they are hearing. Likewise, if you feel that you are somewhat defensive when facing a negotiation situation, you can monitor your body language to make sure that the messages you are transmitting are the ones that you expose in words and that you are open and receptive to what is discussed.

Working with groups: disconnection

Have you ever found yourself presenting a project and had the feeling that your audience was not interested in what you were saying? Have you ever found yourself having to lead a team to reach a consensus on responsibilities and deadlines? Was everyone lined up to come up with a solution, or was there some disconnect between team members?

Ideally, when you have to make a presentation or work with a group, you want 100% participation by everyone. This does not always happen, and sometimes it is necessary to involve the audience, for this act, you must identify the signs of their "disconnection":

- Low heads.
- Staring or distracting with other things.
- Hands playing with clothes or pencils.
- People may be writing or scribbling.
- They may be sitting sunk in their chairs.

When you identify that someone doesn't seem to be involved in what's going on, you can do something to get him or her back on track and focus on the topic of the meeting again, for example, by asking them a direct question.

And while all this is happening, don't forget that your own body must also show the confidence and security you want it to express.

Detect the lie

Of all the non-verbal body language that we can observe, being able to perceive whether a person is lying or not, puts us in a very good position. Some of the signs that indicate when someone is lying are:

- The eyes maintain little or no contact, there are usually rapid movements of the eyes, and the pupils are constricted.
- The hands or fingers are in front of the mouth when speaking.
- The body turns physically away from you, or there are unusual/unnatural body gestures.
- Increase in breathing rate.
- Changes in skin tone, turning red on the face or neck.
- Increase in perspiration.
- Changes in voice, such as a change in tone, stuttering, or clearing their throat.

It is important to remember that each person's body language is slightly different. If you do not find any of these signs, you must not tiptoe what your interlocutor is saying, nor the contrary. Even if you identify some of them, it does not always mean that they are lying, they can be a reflection of other symptoms, such as nervousness.

What you can do is use these signs as a claim, to go deeper into the subject and thus get out of doubt. Asking for more details on some issues is always helpful to contrast the information with the person's body language, especially in job interviews and in negotiation situations.

Interpretation of body language: do not fall into generalizations

We have already mentioned that each person is unique and that their signs and signals could have a different underlying cause than we suspect. This is usually the case when people have different past experiences, and especially when the cultural differences are great. For this reason, it is important to check that our interpretation of body language is correct.

You can do this by asking new questions, but it will be important for your body language to help the other person open up. To develop and put into practice body language interpretation skills, it is important to observe people: on the bus or television (removing the sound), trying to find out what they are saying, or what relationship there is between them.

Although you may never know if your assumptions are true, this exercise will help you pick up signals when you are interacting with other people.

And remember, if you need to convey confidence: eye contact, open posture, and smile. It never fails!

CHAPTER 14

THE SUBCONSCIOUS MIND AND THE LIMBIC BRAIN SYSTEM

Accumulated fears, beliefs, and previous experience largely determine our future, and that is why we need to work with our subconscious. Together with a specialist, Maria Samarina, we try to understand the issue.

Our brain is stunning—its capabilities have not been explored to the tenth. But what we already know about it allows us to manage our own life, to create it of our own free will. We can change our reality by influencing the subconscious, and this is not fiction at all.

Where do consciousness and subconsciousness live?

For our mind—logic, knowledge, and thought process—our consciousness is responsible. It is concentrated in the neocortex, the largest part of the brain. The same one, with convolutions. It is with the help of the neocortex that we read, write, solve logical problems, set goals, and think through strategies. While we are awake, the consciousness is with us, and in a dream it also rests.

The subconscious mind hides deeper—in the reptilian mind and limbic system. These parts of the brain are billions of years older than the neocortex. Therefore, the subconscious mind does not understand human speech. It only responds to images, emotions, and bodily sensations.

Initially, the task of the subconscious mind was to ensure survival; therefore, it stores all the information that a person receives throughout life, without sorting it at all—what if it comes in handy and helps the owner? The subconscious does not need rest; it always works.

When compared to a computer, consciousness is RAM, and the subconscious is a hard drive of infinite volume. All information that falls into the subconscious is processed by it and stored later in the form of programs—ready-made options for a person's reaction. Remember that it seeks to make our lives easier? In the future, we act according to the schemes.

You once burned your hand grabbing a hot pot—now you come to all pots with a towel. A boy you liked laughed at you when you first went skating—and now you don't like the rink, even if you learned to ride.

96% of what we call our personality, all our habits, fears, addictions, spontaneous reactions, are determined by the subconscious mind—that part of the brain that we do not control.

How programs are formed

How is the formation of programs (or attitudes) of the subconscious? Information in the form of a nerve impulse is transmitted to the brain through chains of neural connections. They are created and destroyed constantly. The more often the same information arrives, the stronger these chains become. There is a "beaten path"—a steady program of the subconscious. That is why repetition becomes the easiest way to get hold of the installation.

Most often, they turn out to be strangers, especially if acquired in childhood. It is at this age that we are most susceptible to the opinions of other people. What parents, relatives, or teachers inspire in us for many years defines our life. Well, if a child was told that he is capable, that he is loved and appreciated, then he is more likely to grow a confident person and not be afraid to do something new.

But phrases like "you are not given," "you are so stupid," or "you can't do anything" can easily give rise to future failure and fears just because the subconscious will be programmed like that.

We perfectly take root settings with the help of emotions. Children's fears can interfere with the rest of their lives for many years. Even if an adult knows that this is nonsense, he still tries to walk, for example, without stepping on cracks in the asphalt. Or does not like to fall asleep in the dark. Everyone knows that there is no real danger here, but anxiety remains.

How to deal with harmful programs?

Changing the settings of the subconscious, we reprogram the brain. Since the information will be processed using a different algorithm, we will get a different result. It turns out, changing our beliefs, and changing our whole life.

First, identify the settings that bother you the most. It's not hard. Almost all have a lot of restrictive programs. For instance:

- To Earn A Lot, You Need to Work Hard
- Big Money Can Only Be Stolen
- There Is Always Little Money
- Talent Is A Rarity, And Without It, Success Is Impossible
- In Our City (Village) There Is No Good Work

- A Woman Should... (And A Million Options, What Exactly)
- A Man Should... (Similar)
- There Are No Good Men/Women
- Luck Is Not For Me
- No One Can Be Trusted
- I'm Not Good Enough To...
- Ashamed to Have / not have something

You can write a list of several hundred installations! Think about which ones of yours—these or others? What do you want to replace them with? Try on a new program—do you feel warm from it? Listen to the sensations, and you should be comfortable.

If you want to replace programs, you need to be prepared for the resistance of your brain. This is not an easy job. The subconscious mind seeks to preserve everything that has been accumulated, so just a strong-willed effort here is not effective—you have to fight with yourself. Affirmations, if you simply pronounce or read them without using special techniques, will not help either—the subconscious of words does not understand, remember?

How to Speed-Read People

Sooner or later, everyone comes to the idea that it would be good to know how to speed read a person.

Because it allows you to be, if not one step ahead, then at least not one step behind. If someone is trying to deceive, and you know how to recognize a lie, then you can protect yourself from the sad consequences of deception.

<u>Example No. 1.</u> A person asks to borrow money and promises to return it, but if you notice the gestures of lies and understand for yourself that a person is lying, then you can refuse a loan without remorse. This is not even saving, but the safety of one's money, which is usually obtained with difficulty.

<u>Example No. 2.</u> The head suggests heading the department on unfavorable conditions and voices that there are no alternatives. But if you can read a person like a book, and notice that the leader is nervous, you can assume that there are alternatives and begin to agree on the best conditions for themselves.

Reading a person like a book is not so much a dream in modern society as a necessity for those who communicate with people! And it doesn't matter where you communicate: at home, on a date, at work or somewhere else. During communication, people have gestures and facial expressions that say a lot.

Some believe that there are gestures of lies—

gestures that indicate a person's lies and, having seen these gestures, you can find out when a person is lying, and when he is telling the truth.

Others believe that there are facial expressions of lies—facial expressions and micro expressions that help to recognize a lie.

Gestures of lies

Alan Pease and several other authors wrote about poses and gestures. They wrote a lot about lies in particular. However, they were mistaken in many ways. They could not give much that was known for a long time in neuro-linguistic programming.

For example, Pisa has a collection of so-called "closed poses," which supposedly indicate that a person is closed to communication or critical. The simplest and most obvious thing that comes to mind is to use the knowledge of people reading Pisa against themselves: close the position—the person changes communication, thinking that you are critical.

Some people think that touching your nose, eyes, or ears during an explanation always means it is a lie. This is nonsense!

Touching any part of the body is not always a sign of lies. This can be a symptom of a disease (scabies, acute respiratory infections, mental illness). It can be a manipulative gesture or simply an unconscious movement that is not related to the topic of the conversation. There are many options. It's funny when people read a small book and believe that they know everything about a lie, and everyone knows about a person's gestures, including lies. Not just funny - funny!

It's even funnier when such people participate in talk shows on TV channels.

Facial expressions of lies

Paul Ekman became famous for studying facial expressions. It was his life that formed the basis of the plot of The Theory of Lies (rumored). It would seem that here it is - the whole person's face is accessible, and the question of how to read a person will no longer be. But the first 5 minutes of talking with people show that in people, during communication, the face moves as smartly as the leaves of trees in the wind, and this is very confusing.

It seems that many micro expressions are visible and macro expressions too. But there are so many of them that there is often the disappointment that what is described in books is not at all like the reality.

By the way, most books do not describe very, very much.

For example, when a person lies because he believes in lies, or because now the mood is lying in jest, or because of resentment, or something else, is it considered a lie, and how can it be noticed at all?

And how do you recognize a lie by voice, if you get acquainted with pointers (markers) of lies in books? No way. This can only be heard live. When a person lies, his voice changes, his voice can flinch, stammer, and in other ways give lies. It is useful to know what to notice, and even more important to be able to notice it, especially for cases of communication by phone or Skype (vibera and so on), when you only hear a person. It's like reading people's minds, only you are not reading their minds at all, but rather the ideas that are hidden behind the phrases voiced. Moreover, it is important to be able, not to know! Books provide knowledge, and skills give training under the supervision of a professional.

How to find out if a person is lying if the person is not visible and not heard? It can actually be done. There is a technology that allows you to find a lie in the content of words. It is useful to be able to identify a lie in the content of words or the text if you conclude contracts, for example. Not to mention the analysis of the words of politicians, sellers, and many others.

By the way, in very rare cases, lies can be defined outside the meaning of words, without sounds, without seeing a person.

If you remember that people do not always lie, then how do you read people's thoughts and feelings? People have thoughts and emotions, and they may want to hide them, rather than deceive others about how they feel and think. This is not a lie!

Example No. 1. The girl was offended by her boyfriend because he forgot that they had been dating for six months. She may not tell him anything, but her resentment can be noticed. If the guy notices on time, then he can talk and apologize or otherwise correct the annoying misunderstanding. And if he doesn't notice, the scandal smells like bonfires.

Example No. 2. The guy is not ready to actively get closer to the girl and does not want to get together with her. But she talks nonstop about plans for living together, describing where the furniture will be, where the children will be, and so on. Perhaps in time, he would have agreed, but not now. In such a situation, her dreamy songs about the future will repel the guy, the tension in the beginning of the relationship will increase, and the negative will firmly bond with the girl.

<u>Example No. 3. </u>It is necessary to agree with the person that he should do some work (issue the necessary document, or sign it, and so on). When there are several such people, a choice arises – whom to approach? People who know how to read a person's train of thoughts and emotions often choose those people who are more likely to perform the actions they need. From the outside, it looks like a "good choice," but the matter is only in the technological determination of the right person.

So, how to speed read a person?

You need to be able to notice what is happening with emotions, mood, and everything else! To know that this is possible, to know what some kind of lips, some kind of forehead, or some pose will say about mood and emotions! Namely, to be able to read a person!

Literally, "I notice that something is not right," even with the slightest muscle movement on the face, subtle at first glance (and at the second too). The ability to recognize a lie and read a person like a book is easy to develop in a couple of days of training.

Is it possible to read a person like a book in ordinary, everyday situations? Not just possible, but necessary!

Situation 1. You come with a company of 5 people to a cafe to order food, and you have little time (an hour). The waiter offers you dishes, mentioning the cooking speed of 20 minutes. It seems that he didn't lie—a fresh dish in their establishment can certainly be ready in 20 minutes, but only one of those ordered! The rest of the people in your friendly company will be forced to wait. As a result, someone will already finish eating, and someone will just start, and someone will generally swallow saliva, and remain hungry.

Situation 2. You are on a date, and the person with whom you spend time is trying in every way to please you. Or just portray sympathy? As long as you do not know how to determine this, you are blind! You rely on your feelings (including intuition), and feelings can fail. Skills are more reliable, but only when they are good. Without them, dates are held in the "it seems like it" mode, but for many, they end unsuccessfully. It's a shame to spend time and money on a person to whom you are indifferent, right? How to understand what you like? To be able to read a person like a book, you must pay attention to his mood, emotions, condition, and train of thought. Without skills, there is only the impression of clarity—the illusion of understanding the situation.

Situation 3. Your child screams and cries in every possible way. Is the parent worried because the child is in trouble, or is it a blatant hysteria for the sake of getting candy, toys, cartoons, and everything else? A parent who does not know how to determine emotions, in almost all cases accurately, goes towards the child, becoming an obedient ward of a small trainer. Further, the child is called "howls of rope" from the parent and "sits on the neck." Most often, such a child's tantrum ends up with problems for the parent and the child.

The most powerful techniques you can use to fake your body language and manipulate Anyone's

The most typical question is, "Is it possible to fake one's body language?" The usual answer to this question is negative because you will give out contradictions between gestures. For example, open palms are associated with honesty, but when a deceiver opens his arms to you and smiles at you, at the same time telling a lie, the micro signals of his body will give out his secret thoughts, such as narrowed pupils, raised eyebrow or curvature of the corner of his mouth. And all these signals will contradict open arms and a wide smile. A person is inclined not to believe what he hears.

There are cases when body language is specially trained to achieve a favorable impression. Consider, for example, Miss America or Miss Universe beauty contests, in which each contestant is trained in such body movements, which radiate warmth and sincerity. The more skillfully a contestant can transmit these signals, the more points she will receive from the judges. But even experienced specialists can imitate the necessary movements only for a short period because soon the body will involuntarily transmit signals that contradict its conscious actions.

Many politicians are experienced specialists in the field of copying body language and use this to get the favor of their voters and make them believe their speeches. They do it successfully, and they say that they have a "divine gift." The face is more often than any other part of the human body used to hide false statements. We smile, nod and wink in an attempt to hide the lie, but, unfortunately for us, our body speaks the truth with its signs, and there is a mismatch between the signals read from the face and body, and words.

Studying facial expressions is an art in itself. It is difficult to imitate and fake body language for a long period, but it is useful to learn how to use positive, open gestures for successful communication with other people and to get rid of gestures that have a negative connotation.

This will make you feel more comfortable in the company of people and will make you more attractive to them.

The problem with the lie is that the subconscious mind works automatically and independently of the person; therefore, body language gives people away. That is why it is immediately noticeable when people who rarely tell a lie, try to lie, no matter how convincingly they present it. At the very moment when he begins to lie, the body begins to give opposite signals, which gives a sense of the speaker's lies. Some people's professions are directly related to deception in various forms, such as politicians. Lawyers, actors, and television commentators have trained their movements to such an extent that it is difficult for people to notice that they are telling a lie and people fall for their bait, and trust them.

They train their gestures in two ways. First, they work out the gestures that give credibility to what was said. But this is only possible if one practices lying for a long period. Secondly, they almost eliminate gestures so that neither positive nor negative gestures are present at the moment they lie. But to do this is very, very difficult.

You can experiment—deliberately tell a lie to your friend and make a deliberate attempt to suppress all kinds of body movements. You are in a full review of your interlocutor. Even if a liar deliberately restrains bright, catchy gestures, the body will somehow transmit a lot of tiny micro signals.

This can be either a curvature of the facial muscles, an expansion or narrowing of the pupils, perspiration on the forehead, a blush on the cheeks, rapid blinking, and many other small gestures that signal fraud. Only people, such as professional interviewers during a conversation, experienced business people during negotiations, and those people who, as we say, have developed intuition, can notice them. The best interviewers and salespeople are such people.

How to Influence and Subdue the Mind

Before you begin, it is important to note that none of these methods are intended to influence other people with obscure intent. Anything that could be harmful to someone in any way, especially their self-esteem, is not included here. These are ways of making friends and influencing people who use psychology positively and without making someone feel bad.

1. Benjamin Franklin effect

We can get someone to do us a favor using a trick, and this is also known as the Benjamin Franklin effect. Legend has it that when Franklin was in the Pennsylvania Legislative Assembly, there was an opponent who had once spoken against him (Franklin does not say his name), someone very influential. Franklin was very uneasy about this opposition and hatred and decided to win over this gentleman. What occurred to him is very curious and intelligent. Instead of doing this gentleman a favor or service, he induced the opponent to do him a favor by borrowing a rare book from his library. The gentleman in question immediately lent it to him, and Franklin returned it one-week-old with a note in which he greatly appreciated the favor. When they met again in parliament, the gentleman spoke to him (which he had never done before) and, above all, with a great education. From then on, this gentleman was always ready to help Franklin, and they became great friends, a friendship that continued until his death. This fact demonstrates the truth of a maxim that Franklin had learned as a child that says: "It is more likely that someone who has already done a previous one will do you another favor than not one who owes it to you."

There is another very illustrative example of this phenomenon in The Karamazov brothers of Dostoyevsky. Fyodor Pavlovitch recalls how, once in the past, he was asked why he had hated a person so much. And he replied: "I will tell you. He has done me no harm. I was very dirty with him once and have hated him ever since." Just as in these examples, we get a vicious circle, the Benjamin Franklin effect shows that it is also possible to generate virtuous circles.

The scientists decided to test this theory and found that those who were asked by the researcher for a personal favor, made much more favorable assessments of him than the other groups. It may seem contradictory since common sense tells us that we do favors for people we like, and we annoy those we don't like. But the reality seems to be that we tend to like people with whom we are kind and to dislike people with whom we are rude or misbehave ourselves.

2. Too much

The trick Is to ask at first for much more than we want or need to lower our request later. You start by throwing an exaggerated request at someone, and the request will most likely be rejected. He then turns back soon after and wonders about something much less extravagant, which is actually what we wanted in the first place. This trick may also sound counter-intuitive, but the idea behind it is that the person feels bad about denying our first request, even though it was not reasonable. So when they ask for something reasonable, they will feel more compelled to help this time.

3. The proper name

Using a person's name or title, depending on the situation is another tool to gain trust. Dale Carnegie, the author of "How to Win Friends and Influence People" emphasizes this. Listening to us validates our existence and leads us to have more positive feelings about the person who validates us. The use of a title or a nickname can also have very strong effects. This can be as easy as calling an acquaintance and calling him "mate" or "partner" whenever we see him, or referring to a person we want to work with or continue to work with as a "boss." While this might sound quite corny, it works in practice. "How to Win Friends and Influence People" demonstrates why it is incredibly necessary and successful to make friends use someone's name. A person's name is said to be the sweetest sound in any language for that person. The name is the fundamental part of our identity.

4. Flattery

Flattery opens many doors. This may seem obvious at first, but there are some important caveats to be aware of. For starters, it is important to know that if flattery is not seen as sincere, it will do more harm than good. Researchers have studied the motivations and reactions behind flattery and have found some very important things. People tend to seek cognitive balance, always trying to keep their thoughts and feelings organized similarly. So if we flatter someone who has high self-esteem and finds it sincere, they are going to like it very much, as we are validating their feelings. However, if we flatter someone who has low self-esteem, there is a chance that it could backfire, because it interferes with how it is perceived. That, of course, does not mean that we should degrade a person of low self-esteem.

5. Mirroring or the mirror technique

Mirroring, also known as mimicry or mirror technique, is something that some people do naturally. People with this ability are considered "chameleons"; They try to fit in with their surroundings by copying the attitudes, movements, and even speech patterns of other people. This ability, however, can also be used intentionally and is a perfect strategy for becoming more friendly. Researchers studied mimicry and found that those who had been imitated were much more likely to act favorably towards the person who had copied them. Even more interesting was their second finding, that those with someone who mimicked their behavior seemed more interesting and more personable in front of others. Probably the reason this is so is that the reflection of someone's behavior makes them feel validated. This validation is positively associated with feeling greater self-esteem and greater security, more happiness, and feeling a better disposition towards others.

6. The use of fatigue

People are more sensitive to something that anyone can say when they are tired, whether it's a comment or a question. The explanation for this is that mental energy levels drop significantly when people are tired. When we request from someone who is tired, they will probably not have a definitive answer, and we will probably get an "I will do it tomorrow" answer because they do not want to face the decisions at that moment. The next day, they are more likely to be inclined to help us, as people tend to keep their word; it is psychologically natural to want to go ahead with something you said would be done.

7. Offers that cannot be rejected

It consists of starting with a request that they cannot reject. This is a reverse "aim high" technique. Instead of starting with a large order, you start with something very small. Once someone has agreed to help us or agrees with us, they will be more likely to be more receptive to fulfilling a larger request. Scientists tested this phenomenon in advertising. They started by getting people to express their support for the environment and rain forests, which is a fairly simple request. Next, they found that once someone had come to express their agreement to support the environment, it was much easier to convince them to buy products that supported rainforests and whatnot.

8. Know how to correct

Correcting people when they are wrong isn't a smart idea. In his popular novel, Carnegie also pointed out that telling others they're wrong is usually pointless and makes people stay away from us. There is a better way to show disagreement and turn it into a polite conversation without saying they are wrong, as it affects the essence of their ego. The idea behind this is quite simple: instead of arguing, listen to what they have to say, and then try to understand how they feel and why. Then discover the common ground that you share with him and use it as a starting point to explain your position. This makes the other person much more likely to listen to what you have to say and allow you to correct him without losing your position.

9. Repeat things

Repeating something that our interlocutor has just said is one of the most positive ways to influence others, since we show that we understand what they are saying to us and how they feel, thus manifesting our empathy. One of the most effective ways to do this is to paraphrase what they say and repeat it, also known as reflective listening. Studies have shown that when therapists use reflective listening, people tend to reveal their emotions more and have a better therapeutic relationship. This can be transferred by talking to our friends. If we listen to what they tell us and rephrase it as a question to confirm that we understand it, they will feel more comfortable talking to us. They will also show more friendship and will be more likely to listen to what we have to say, as it showed that we care about them.

10. To agree

This involves nodding as we talk, particularly when we want to ask for a favor. Scientists have found that people are more likely to agree with the other person when they nod while listening to something. They have also seen that when someone nods a lot in front of us, we end up doing the same. This is understandable because human beings are well known for imitating behaviors, especially those that we consider having a positive connotation. So if you want to be very convincing, nod regularly throughout the conversation. The person who is speaking will find it difficult not to agree, and they will begin to feel good vibrations towards what is being said, without even knowing it.

CHAPTER 15

HOW TO USE SUBLIMINAL MESSAGES AND HOW TO USE THEM TO MANIPULATE PEOPLE

Do you want your life to embrace new possibilities? Want to widen the horizons and crack the walls around you?

The power of subliminal messages is still to be discovered.

The Subliminal Messages Force-What Is It?

Subliminal signals act like magic wands. Wield them, and things are going to go your way unexpectedly, miraculously, and you don't even have to expend too much effort to control things. And that works on all facets of your life, including your job, financial status, personal and professional aspirations, dating, social life, etc. Your life is plentiful, and full, and you don't need to break your back to make that difference.

Subliminal messages in videos make all of that possible with one strong weapon: your subconscious.

Sounds almost surreal? Well, numerous experiments and trials have proved and tested the phenomenon. If you need to be convinced, here's a short response to the question, "How do subliminal messages work?"

How Do Subliminal Messages Work?

Subliminal signals are brief or secret orders in music, videos, and other artistic mediums. Their primary aim is to influence a person from within or the subconscious outwardly. Instead of actively forcing you to change your mind, the messages cultivate, strengthen, or improve subconscious-level thoughts to facilitate the change from deep within your mind. This is more powerful as it can change habits and control thoughts and emotions that we don't have full control over sometimes.

You do not hear or see any subliminal video messages while listening to subliminal music or viewing subliminal videos; these function very stealthily, in secret, and can be understood only by the subconscious mind.

And the best thing about them is that they function even without your understanding, so you won't be able to combat the messages' impact with harmful habits of thinking that we can't keep out of our minds at times.

Subliminal video messages, when used correctly, hold

power over everything you have ever wanted to achieve in life. And even if they don't make all that you want to materialize, the messages can create such a perfect and content state of mind in you so that you can see things positively and powerfully.

Is there anything you'd like to achieve? Make sure that you have a chance for subliminal video messages.

Do subliminal messages work fast?

Now, the next question is, "Do subliminal messages work fast?" What if your next day's coming up with an exam or a big job interview? What if you give a really important client a presentation? What if you're about to sign a big deal? What if you're sick of life, and want more? How long do you have to wait until you can experience the beautiful impact of subliminal video messages?

Subliminal messages are often used, mentally or otherwise, as remedies or therapies for different problems. They can help with weight loss, sleep disorder recovery, depression, anxiety, phobia, trauma, stress, and so on, for example. And they are highly successful and helpful because in only a few days they are not only healthy and normal but also known to start having positive effects.

Listening to subliminal music or watching videos will make you experience the impact right afterward. But if you want the optimistic state of mind to be a constant in your life, cultivating the habit of the subliminal message will cause changes in your life in no time!

How to Decode Micro Expressions

Under the influence of feelings experienced by a person, coordinated contractions and relaxation of various facial structures are born. They define a facial expression that perfectly reflects the emotions experienced. Since it is not difficult to learn how to control the condition of the facial muscles, the display of emotions on the face is often tried to mask, or even imitate. Knowing facial expressions with different emotions is useful not only to understand others but also for the most thorough working out of your working imitations.

The sincerity of human emotions is usually indicated by symmetry in displaying feelings on the face. The stronger the falsity, the more different are the facial expressions of its right and left halves.

Even easily recognizable facial expressions are sometimes very short-lived (fractions of a second) and often go unnoticed; to be able to intercept it, you

165

need practice or special training. At the same time, positive emotions (joy, pleasure) are recognized more easily than negative ones (sadness, shame, disgust).

The lips of a person are distinguished by special emotional expressiveness, which is not difficult to read. For example, enhanced facial expressions or biting the lips, for example, indicate anxiety, and a mouth twisted to one side indicates skepticism or ridicule.

A smile on the face usually shows friendliness or a need for approval. A smile for a man is a good opportunity to show that he owns himself in any situation. A woman's smile is much more truthful and more often corresponds to her actual mood. Since smiles very often reflect different motives, it is advisable not to rely too much on their standard interpretation:

- Excessive smile - a need for approval;
- Crooked smile - a sign of controlled nervousness;
- A smile with raised eyebrows - a willingness to obey;
- A smile with lowered eyebrows - showing superiority;

- A smile without lifting the lower eyelids - insincerity;
- A smile with a constant expansion of the eyes without closing them is a threat.

Typical facial expressions that report experiencing emotions are:

Joy: lips are curved, and their corners are pulled back, small wrinkles have formed around the eyes;

Interest: eyebrows are slightly raised or lowered, while the eyelids are slightly widened or narrowed;

Happiness: the outer corners of the lips are raised and usually laid back; eyes are calm;

Surprise: raised eyebrows form wrinkles on the forehead, the eyes are widened, and the parted mouth has a rounded shape;

Disgust: eyebrows are lowered, the nose is wrinkled, the lower lip is protruded or raised and closed with upper lip, eyes are as if mowed; the person as if choked or spits;

Contempt: the eyebrow is raised, the face is extended, the head is raised as if a person is looking down at someone; he is as if removed from the interlocutor;

Fear: eyebrows are slightly raised but have a straight shape, their inner angles are shifted, and horizontal wrinkles pass through the forehead, the eyes are widened, the lower eyelid is tense, and the upper one is slightly raised. The mouth can be opened, and its corners are pulled back, stretching and straightening lips over the teeth (the latter is just talking about the intensity of emotion...); when only the mentioned position of the eyebrows is available, then this is a controlled fear;

Anger: the forehead muscles are shifted inward and downward, organizing a threatening or frowning expression of the eyes, the nostrils are widened, and the wings of the nose are raised. The lips are either tightly compressed or pulled back, taking a rectangular shape and exposing gritted teeth, the face often turns red;

Shame: the head is lowered, the face is turned away, the eyes are averted, the eyes are turned downward or "run" from side to side, the eyelids are covered and sometimes closed; the face is quite reddened, the pulse is rapid, breathing is intermittent;

Grief: the eyebrows are lowered, the eyes are dull, and the outer corners of the lips are sometimes slightly lowered.

Knowing facial expressions with different emotions is useful not only to understand others but also for the most thorough working out (usually in front of a mirror) of your working imitations.

1. Sight and eyes

This openly shows the inner experiences of a person—not without reason experienced "players" try to hide their expression behind the lens of dark glasses.

People are usually given out:

- Any changes in the usual expression of the eyes - the emergence of a certain emotion, a response signal to the stimulus;
- Involuntary eye movements, noticeably "rolling eyes" - anxiety, shame, deceit, fear, neurasthenia;
- Brilliant look - fever, excitement;
- A glazed look - extreme weakness;
- Pupil enlargement - a sense of interest and pleasure from information, communication, photography, partner, food, music, and other external factors, the adoption of something, but also severe suffering;

- Narrowing of the pupils - rolling irritation, anger, hatred, initial negative emotions, rejection of something;
- Chaotic movements of the pupils - a sign of intoxication (the more such movements, the more drunk a person);
- Increased blinking - agitation, deception.

People always prefer to look at those they admire or at those with whom they have a close relationship, from close range, while women show greater visual interest than men.

In the course of communication, they often look at the partner in the eye when they are listening, and not when they are talking. However, when carrying out the suggestion, sometimes they use a direct look in the eye during dialogue.

A person who looks into your eyes noticeably less than one-third of the entire period of communication is either dishonest or trying to hide something; the one who stubbornly stares into the eyes has increased interest in you (the pupils are dilated), shows outright hostility (the pupils are narrowed) or seeks to dominate.

Modifications of eye contacts have the following decoding:

- Absent gaze - focused thinking;
- Looking at the surrounding objects and the ceiling - a drop in interest in the conversation, an unnecessarily long monologue of the partner;
- Persistent gaze in the eyes (pupils narrowed) - a sign of hostility and a clear desire to dominate;
- Persistent gaze in the eyes (pupils dilated) - a sign of sexual interest;
- Looking away and lowering one's eyes - shame, deceit;
- Side view - distrust;
- The gaze is either diverted or now returned - lack of agreement, distrust.

2. Pose and its details

Significant information about the inner mood of a person gives a static position of his body. At the same time, the often-repeated pose informs about the stable personality traits.

Since people usually have better control over their face than the body in the extremes of feelings, it's often not a facial expression at all, but a pose that can tell about the individual's true experiences.

Possible bindings of body positions to the mental state of a person are as follows:

- Hands clasped behind the back, head high, chin up - a feeling of self-confidence and superiority over others;
- The body is forward, hands (akimbo) on the hips - self-confidence and willingness to take action, aggressiveness, over-agitation during a conversation, the desire to defend one's position to the end;
- Standing with your hands on a table or chair - a feeling of the incompleteness of contact with a partner;
- Hands with apart elbows wound behind the head - awareness of superiority over others;
- Putting your thumbs in your belt or the slit in your pockets is a sign of aggressiveness and demonstrated self-confidence;
- Protruding thumbs from pockets - a sign of superiority;
- Crossed limbs - skeptical protective installation;
- Non-crossed limbs and an unbuttoned jacket - the establishment of trust;
- Tilting the head to the side - an awakening of interest;

- Head tilt down - negative attitude;
- The slight deviation of the head back is a sign of aggressiveness;
- Sitting on the edge of the chair - the willingness to jump up at any moment to either leave, or act in the current situation, or to calm down the accumulated excitement, or to attract attention and connect to the conversation;
- Throwing one leg on the other with arms crossed on the chest - a sign of "disconnection" from the conversation;
- Throwing a foot on the arm of a chair (sitting on it) - neglect of others, loss of interest in the conversation;
- Crossed ankles of a seated person - restraint of disapproving attitude, fear or agitation, the attempt of self-control, negative protective state;
- Position (sitting or standing) with legs oriented toward the exit - a clear desire to end the conversation and leave;
- Frequent change of poses, fidgeting in a chair, fussiness - inner anxiety, tension;
- Getting up is a signal that a decision has been made, the conversation is tiring, something surprised or shocked;

173

- Finger grip - frustration and the desire to hide a negative attitude (the higher the hands are located at the same time, the stronger the negative);
- The tips of the fingers connect the hands, but the palms are not in contact - a sign of superiority and confidence in oneself and one's words;
- Hands rest with elbows on the table, and their hands are located in front of the mouth - hiding their true intentions, playing with a partner in cat and mouse;
- Supporting the head with a palm - boredom;
- Fingers clenched in a fist are located under the cheek, but do not serve to support the head - a sign of interest;
- Propping up the chin with the thumb is a sign of some critical assessment;
- Clasping his glass with two hands - masked nervousness;
- Smoke upward from a cigarette - a positive attitude, self-confidence;
- Blowing smoke from a cigarette down is a negative mood, with hidden or suspicious thoughts.

3. Gestures and body movements

"A gesture is not a movement of the body, but a movement of the soul." It reports on the desire of the person and what he is experiencing at a particular moment, and the gesture familiar to someone indicates the trait of his character. Externally, the same gestures of different people can mean completely different things, but there are identical moments:

- Active gesturing is a frequent component of positive emotions, understood by others as showing friendliness and interest;
- Excessive gesticulation is a sign of anxiety or insecurity.
- When determining the thoughts and emotions of an individual, only involuntary gestures should be noted:
- Open hands demonstration - an indicator of frankness;
- Clenching of fists - internal arousal, aggressiveness (the stronger the fingers clench, the stronger the emotion itself);
- Covering your mouth with your hand (or glass in your hand) at the time of speech - surprise, uncertainty in the spoken, lies, confidential

message, professional safety net from reading lips;

- Touching the nose or lightly scratching it - insecurity in the message (both by yourself and the partner), a lie, a search for a new counterargument during the discussion;
- Rubbing the eyelid with a finger indicates a lie, but sometimes - a feeling of suspicion and lies on the part of the partner;
- Rubbing and scratching various fragments of the head (forehead, cheeks, nape, ear) - concern, embarrassment, uncertainty;
- Stroking the chin - the moment of decision making;
- The fussiness of the hands (pulling something, twisting and untwisting a fountain pen, touching parts of clothing) - alertness, nervousness, embarrassment;
- Pinching the palm - readiness for aggression;
- Biting nails - internal anxiety;
- All kinds of movements of the arm across the body (adjust the watch, touch the cufflink, play with the button on the cuff) - masked nervousness;
- Picking up villi from clothes is a gesture of disapproval;

- Pulling from the neck a disturbing collar - a person suspects that others have recognized his deception, lack of air with anger;
- Rubbing the glasses or placing the temples of their frames in their mouths - a pause for reflection, please wait;
- Removing points and throwing them on the table is an overly sharp conversation, a difficult and unpleasant topic;
- Quenching or snoozing - the period of maximum stress;
- Knocking down ashes from a cigarette too often - a painful internal state, nervousness;
- Tilting the head to one side - awakening interest;
- A quick tilt or turn of the head to the side - the desire to speak out;
- The constant casting of supposedly "interfering" hair from the forehead is a concern;
- A clear desire to lean on something or lean against something - a sense of complexity and unpleasantness of the moment, a lack of understanding of how to get out of the situation (any support increases self-confidence).

Body Language Mistakes to Avoid

Body language plays an important role in the communication process. Our postures and movements while communicating with other people, can both improve one's opinion about us and worsen it.

It is logical that, in this case, you need to work on yourself and concentrate around controlling your gestures. But there is one caveat: as a rule, habits associated with the "wrong" body language are very difficult to eradicate. We don't even notice how often we look away, cross our arms, or stoop for no reason.

Let us now pay attention at least to the main mistakes in facial expressions and gestures, because of which everyone has problems. If you can get rid of them, then this will make your communication much more productive.

1. Fussiness

If nervous fussiness has become a habit, then it will be hard for you to abandon it.

When you fuss, you show nervousness and weakness.

It would help if you learned to control this bad habit.

2. Game with hair

You do not know where to put your hands and constantly reach for your head to wind a lock of hair on your finger? From the outside, it looks very incomprehensible. Also, because of this, you cannot focus on the conversation. In the end, you not only spoil your hair but run the risk of harming your hair. Therefore, it is better not to touch them at all.

3. Closed poses

If you cross your arms over your chest, this is interpreted as an attempt to distance yourself from reality and protect yourself. But many people perceive this as a comfortable pose, which is easiest to take if you don't know where to put your hands.

Nevertheless, all protective postures have negative consequences. Crossed arms and tightness make us unconvincing and cause suspicion of the interlocutor.

Body Language Specialist Patti Wood says: "You need to keep your hands in sight during the conversation. When the interlocutor does not see your hands, he thinks that you are trying to conceal something."

4. Gestures too active

People have different attitudes to the use of gestures.

Someone may not gesture at all during a conversation, but someone else may spin in different directions and constantly wave his arms.

In this case, the main role is played by a person's temperament. But at the same time, experts say that gesturing is the most effective way to draw public attention to your words. But here it is very important to avoid gestures that discredit you.

You can't poke your finger, imagine yourself in the role of a conductor, and use dance moves.

5. Uncertain gait

People are prone to pickiness and strict criticism. We are confident that we can learn everything about the interlocutor, making conclusions only based on his manner of walking.

According to statistics, our walk even affects the risk of being robbed on the street. Therefore, it is important to make your walking style more refined and coordinated. This is not an easy task, but you can't walk shuffling all the time.

6. Lack of a smile

We often underestimate the importance of a smile and even consider that a smile for no reason is a sign of cunning and hypocrisy. Sometimes we are proud that in dealing with people, we constantly use the so-called "poker face."

We use the phrase "on-duty smile," by which we mean something insincere and false. So far, there is no need to talk about social politeness at all. But in many other countries, a smile is appreciated very highly. So a sincere smile can be of great benefit to you.

A laid-back smile is a sign not only of friendliness but also of confidence, honesty, warmth, and affection for a person. Do not forget that a smile has a mirror effect and makes the interlocutor smile back. If you do not smile, then you look detached and gloomy.

7. Distraction for extraneous things

Most of all, people are annoyed when the interlocutor does not pay due attention to them during a conversation. Sometimes people get distracted for a good reason. Sometimes they have important things that they cannot postpone for later.

Nevertheless, in most cases, they check the mail, unsubscribe to friends in instant messengers or leaf through the feed-in social networks. If you are in company, it is better to learn to restrain yourself from these impulses. Otherwise, they will begin to consider you impolite and disinterested in them.

8. Stoop

Straighten your back! Bad posture can occur out of the blue, especially when you spend most of the day in the office at your desk.

Stooping not only makes us look insecure but also harms our backs. After abandoning it, you will benefit in two ways: take care of your health and improve your reputation in the eyes of others.

9. Averted eyes or aggressive gaze

This is one of the most common mistakes, moderation, and meaningfulness of actions that will help get rid of it. The author of the book, "What your body says," Sharon Sailer believes that the perfect eye contact of the interlocutors implies a series of long glances and not a game of peepers.

If you look into the interlocutor's eyes for too long without looking away, you make him feel awkward. At the same time, the desire to avoid eye contact indicates insecurity and even contempt.

10. Excessive calm

This is still better than an emotional explosion,

violent gestures, or energetic movements in the process of business negotiations. But you still don't need to become like a statue, because otherwise, the interlocutor will think that you are not interested in the conversation.

It's worth using mirror tactics. No, you do not need to completely copy the gestures and facial expressions of another person, as he may be offended by this. Carefully repeat the main gestures, maintaining the proper level of expression. Proper mirroring will make you seem positive and confident.

Refusing stone expression and making your facial expressions natural is a difficult task, especially for those who, by nature, are not emotional and open people. But efforts will bring good results.

CONCLUSION

Our nonverbal or body language is one of the most powerful forms of communication that we use in our day-to-day experiences. It is the contact mode that ignites our emotions and responses at the "healthy level." Research has shown that having an understanding of body language improves one's potential to be effective in getting out of any given situation whatever one wants.

Have you ever seen a couple sitting together and had a sense of just how good or bad their relationship was in minutes? Have you ever wondered how you could arrive so easily at this conclusion without any direct interaction? If you are aware of it or not, we spend our days listening to non-verbal signs of people interpreted by their body language and drawing conclusions from our assumptions about them.

Our body language shows the reality that we conceal from the world with our expressions, including our feelings towards ourselves, our relationships, and our circumstances. The people we associate with will evaluate our motives, the strength of our relationships, how masterful we are in any given circumstance, our level of trust, and what our true motivations and desires are through our eye contact, movements, body posture, and facial expressions.

The strength of body language is contained in the resulting emotional reaction. In nearly every situation, emotions influence decisions and reactions. Non-verbal signals trigger emotions that define an individual's core assets, such as truthfulness, trustworthiness, honesty, skill level, and capacity to lead. The perception of these signals will decide who we are going to meet, the work we are being hired for, what degree of success we are having, and even who will be elected to powerful political positions.

Why don't we spend years studying and improving successful body language abilities with such an essential skill? The truth is that most people underestimate the importance of body language before they try a deeper understanding of human actions in a personal relationship, or gain an edge in a competitive business setting.

Mastery in body language provides the keys for people to perceive the context behind particular movements and body movement, as well as to provide an understanding of how to project and convey messages while communicating with others effectively. The cumulative success of interpersonal partnerships is, therefore, significantly improved. The best way to start this learning process is to learn the basic understanding of the two styles of core body language-open presence and closed presence.

The closed body language form of presence is found in individuals who fold their bodies around the centerline of the body, which runs straight down the middle of the body from the top of the head to the feet. The physical features that produce this form of appearance are feet positioned next to each other, arms held close to the chest, hands crossed on the chest or held together in front of the body, slight hand movements kept close to the body, shoulders rolled forward and eyes fixed below eye level.

The signals sent to the world by the body language form of closed presence are a lack of confidence, low self-esteem, powerlessness, and lack of experience. In extreme cases, the message of wanting to be invisible may even be produced. The consequences of this kind of body language on the person projecting can range from simply not having the best possible opportunities to a worst-case scenario of harboring a self-fulfilling image of victimization.

The open presence, by comparison, is featured in individuals who build a sense of authority, control, and leadership by projecting mastery of confidence, achievement, energy, and ability. The physical

186

features are feet held hip apart, open hand movements used in speech away from the body's centerline, elbows held away from the chest, shoulders pulled back, upright postures and eyes fixed on their listeners' eye level. These individuals are viewed as desirable, competent, intelligent, and are easily seen as having success. We see this form of body language as the 'leaders' body language.'

The secret is eye contact to develop body language and to start projecting an open presence. Eye contact is one of the social devices that we own most. Someone can alter the way others see them by using direct eye contact while communicating with others. When people start looking directly into the eyes of an individual, they are seen as confident, trustworthy, and professional.

Hand movements and facial expressions are the second forms of transition that one can render with accessible presence to be seen. Both modes of communication improve the ability to efficiently convey messages. Through skillfully using open hand gestures away from the body and expressive facial expression, the greater impact is produced while speaking making the audience more visually relaxed and increasing the amount of information presented during the conversation.

As kids, we are told from an early age that healthy boys and girls sit together correctly with legs and hands crossed in front of them. The desire to restrict physical space as children will establish some of the characteristics of the closed presence at adulthood found in body language. To combat this effect, one can start adopting the characteristics of body language of the open presence and integrating these manners into one's natural state of being. After this behavioral shift has been achieved, it should have the same non-verbal experiences and signals as its counterpart's inaccessible contact.

Body language mastery is essential to creating the most powerful presence in all interpersonal interactions. Individuals lacking this knowledge are vulnerable to confusion and find their attempts inadequate in expressing their ideas. With the ability to distinguish between the various body language styles, everybody can achieve the mastery required to succeed in whatever endeavor they want.

www.ingramcontent.com/pod-product-compliance
Ingram Content Group UK Ltd.
Pitfield, Milton Keynes, MK11 3LW, UK
UKHW021418210125
4213UKWH00032B/457